T0012221

THE ESSENCE OF FORM

AARON KREINBROOK

THE ESSENCE OF FORM

© 2024, Aaron Kreinbrook

Print ISBN: 979-8-35094-748-9
eBook ISBN: 979-8-35094-749-6

CONTENTS

1. INTRODUCTION 1

2. DEFINITIONS 2

3. IMPLICATIONS 4

3.1. CONSCIOUSNESS   4

   3.1.1. PERSPECTIVES   5

   3.1.2. LIMITATIONS   11

3.2. CONSTITUTION   16

   3.2.1. APPEARANCE   16

      3.2.1.1. BOUNDARIES   19

      3.2.1.2. CONTENTS   28

      3.2.1.3. DIMENSIONS   38

      3.2.1.4. INTEGRITY   43

   3.2.2. DISAPPEARANCE   47

3.3. POTENTIAL   49

   3.3.1. EQUILIBRIUM   50

   3.3.2. STATUS   54

3.4. SOURCE   59

   3.4.1. HIERARCHY   60

   3.4.2. TYPES   64

3.5. FUNCTION   69

    3.5.1. PROPRIETY   73

       3.5.1.1. NATURE   75

       3.5.1.2. NATURAL   77

       3.5.1.3. CONTRIVANCES   80

    3.5.2. VALUE   81

1.

INTRODUCTION

True to its title, this book is concerned with the essence of form. In order to understand the essence of form in general, we must, after defining what we mean by "essence" and "form", come to understand universal principles that apply to any form in particular. To this end, five categories applicable to the essence of form are explored herein which we may identify and abstract from five specific questions, or similarly phrased questions, that may be asked of any form in an effort to uncover its essence: 1.) "What is the nature and involvement of the *consciousness* that perceives it?", 2.) "What is its *constitution*?", 3.) "What is its *potential*?", 4.) "What is its *source*?", 5.) "What is its *function*?". When applied to particular forms, these questions are implicit of each other and logically interdependent insofar as the answer to any one question necessitates the answers to the others. Collectively, the answers to these questions serve as the answer to the question "What is the essence of form?", which satisfies the objective of this book.

2.

DEFINITIONS

Let us limit our basic definition of the word "form" to a noun that, at once, signifies 1.) something in particular and 2.) the way that something in particular appears to be. We might identify something in particular simply as a "this" or "that", which implicates its singularly finite existence. We might consider the way that something in particular appears to be in terms of *how* something in particular is, the state of which is implied from its existence and consists of apparent attributes, including behavior, that may be described.

The term "form", as a noun, is commonly associated with objects that are beheld through our senses of sight, touch and sound. Our definition and usage of the term going forward, however, is applicable to anything in particular, which includes, but is not limited to, what is perceived through all of our senses, as every particular thing that exists, in whatever state, is a finite something in particular that has a specific way in which it presents itself to us and our understanding; every particular thing is a form that has an expressed form; every particular thing *is* a form, *has* a form, *does* its form, and is *had* as a form through the existence, ownership and presentation of itself.

The "essence" of anything in particular is defined by its necessary constituents to the extent that any alteration of its necessary constituents would fundamentally change *what* it is, relative to that of other particular things. Form, in general, is not an expendable attribute or property of something in particular, but rather it is a necessary constituent of, and thereby *essential* to, what something in particular *is*, since nothing in particular can *be* without having and expressing a form of some kind. Moreover, the necessary constituents of any particular form, including, as particular forms, the term "form" and its meaning, always align with the basic criteria articulated in our definition of the term "form", namely, that each is something in particular that appears *in a particular way.*

3.

IMPLICATIONS

The existence of any form with its appearance logically implies the existence of five categories that are structural to its essence: 1.) *Consciousness* (that and how a form is perceived), 2.) *Constitution* (that of which a form consists), 3.) *Potential* (what a form can become), 4.) *Source* (causation with respect to a form's existence), and 5.) *Function* (a form's purpose or reason for being). Although the essence of each form relates to these categories in different ways, it should be observed that *existence* is common to each form as the implicit and ontologically concurrent basis of its essence.

3.1. CONSCIOUSNESS

Understanding the essence of any particular form, which fundamentally involves the discernment of its existence and expressed appearance relative to that of other particular forms, requires the *consciousness* of a being that is capable of beholding form in the first place; the existence and appearance of anything begs the question "According to whom does this exist?" and "According to whom does this appear as it does?". For if we say that something exists and appears independently of someone's consciousness such that it cannot be known, then we contradict ourselves and negate our statement because we would at least be conscious of this something that cannot be known *as* something that cannot be known. Similarly, if we say that something doesn't exist, then we, at least, have a consciousness of it *as* something that doesn't exist.

Note that we are considering the term "consciousness" broadly to mean *awareness*, which carries with it some degree of understanding. This awareness, of course, implies something that has it, and it implies a subject about which it is concerned. Thus, every particular form that is beheld by consciousness must participate in the essence of consciousness, as a necessary constituent, by serving as its object of awareness. In the same way, we can conclude that consciousness participates in the essence of every particular form, as a necessary constituent, insofar as the existence and appearance of any form logically implies the existence and appearance of some consciousness that beholds any such form. In short, form and consciousness are essentially interdependent such that every form contributes to the existence of the form of consciousness, which, in turn, contributes to the existence of every form.

3.1.1. PERSPECTIVES

All forms can be categorized as either extrinsic or intrinsic in relation to the extrinsic and intrinsic perspectives of reality that one may occupy in consciousness.

The *extrinsic perspective* is always oriented *outward* relative to the person who occupies it. Through the extrinsic perspective, a person has a fundamental understanding of any particular thing, or set of particular things, as a singular entity, which may be expressed generically as 'this' or 'these'. The extrinsic perspective enables a person to be aware of something in particular while restricting the person's awareness of themselves as someone who is aware of something in particular.

As with the extrinsic perspective, the *intrinsic perspective* is always oriented outward with an awareness of something in particular that is implicitly *other* than the person who occupies the perspective. In this regard, the intrinsic perspective is a kind of offshoot of the extrinsic perspective. What is unique about the intrinsic perspective, however, is that the object of its outward orientation is an *inward* reflection of the person who occupies the perspective. Note that the person who engages in self-reflection, with themselves as the *object* of their awareness, can become aware of themselves as engaged in self-reflection, and they can become aware that they are aware of themselves as engaged in self-reflection, and so on, ad infinitum.

The extrinsic and intrinsic perspectives are interdependent such that each cannot exist or function without the other. A person cannot know the extrinsic perspective as such unless they can become aware of themselves as having this orientation of reality through the intrinsic perspective. Similarly, a person cannot know the intrinsic perspective without the use of itself and the outward orientation of the extrinsic perspective.

There are two kinds of understanding that occur with respect to any particular form through either the extrinsic or intrinsic perspective: passive understanding and active understanding. *Passive understanding* is an awareness of the unqualified existence of things such that the existence of something is objectified simply as a singular "this", so to speak, or "you", or "I", or as some other similarly objectifying term that is unqualified. The passive kind of understanding is termed "passive" because it accepts the appearance of its object as it presents itself without any further application of thought. *Active understanding*, on the other hand, produces a rational relationship between two or more objects that have been understood through passive understanding. Thus, passive understanding must precede active understanding in order to serve as the content of the latter. Both passive and active understanding are utilized through the extrinsic and intrinsic perspectives, which, in turn, are utilized by passive and active understanding, *as each allows the other to operate with respect to the consciousness* of any particular form.

We can observe the cooperation of passive and active understanding in relation to the extrinsic and intrinsic perspectives when we identify something with passive understanding as "this" or "you", using the extrinsic perspective, or ourselves as "I", using the intrinsic perspective, which demonstrates our active understanding of these identifications in relation to our passive understanding of what is *not* "this", or "you", or "I", respectively. As any distinction implies that which it is not, through active understanding we must have both the passive understanding of "this", or "you", or "I" as well as the passive understanding of that which is *other* than "this", or "you", or "I" that are perceived using the extrinsic and intrinsic perspectives.

An *extrinsic form* is perceived through the extrinsic perspective by means of our senses such that it is understood as existing *outside* of ourselves somewhere in the space that surrounds us. Extrinsic forms can only be understood as *physical* phenomena that exist outside of a person's psychology, in light of what is understood as non-physical phenomena that exist within a person's psychology. There is a myriad of examples of extrinsic forms, each of which are considered to be in physical space, outside of the person who perceives them. This includes a person's body, with all of its parts, which is regarded as something that is outside of the person's intangible inside, so to speak. Some extrinsic forms may be directly connected to a person's body as an unnatural or unoriginal extension, while other extrinsic forms may be adjacent or related to a person's body through some affiliated proximity. Most extrinsic forms, however, are experienced as wholly disconnected from the body to some measurable distance in space.

An *intrinsic form* is an entity that is understood through the intrinsic perspective as something that resides *within* us. Intrinsic forms can only be understood as non-physical phenomena that exist within a person's psychology, in light of what is understood as physical phenomena that exist outside of a person's psychology. In contrast with extrinsic forms that exist within physical space, intrinsic forms exist within what we might consider to be mental or psychological space, which has an apparently infinite expanse from any point in all directions. Examples of intrinsic forms include anything that is imagined by the human mind or otherwise identified as something that cannot be found through sense perception to exist in the physical environment.

Note that intrinsic forms can be considered as extrinsic forms when a person fails to realize through self-reflection that what they are experiencing is happening within their mind through their understanding, as in a dream, hallucination, or otherwise inaccurate distinction between physical and non-physical reality. Moreover, extrinsic forms could be considered as intrinsic forms when a person understands through self-reflection that their sense perceptions are ultimately mental phenomena that are unavoidably experienced, with some degree of awareness and certainty, as external to themselves. This conclusion seems to be one that contains and locks all of reality within the mind of the human being, although it logically implies something that exists beyond the mind of the human being, and, consequently, negates itself as a complete conclusion.

A person's mind, with its immaterial contents of thoughts and emotions, is an intrinsic form from the person's perspective of themselves; no person can logically objectify their individual mind as if it were something with existence outside of, and apart from, themselves. The minds of other people who are naturally considered to be outside of ourselves are also intrinsic forms within us, although they are not experienced as such, viz., as contained within our minds; the minds of other people are treated with their bodies as extrinsic forms, even though we cannot observe their minds, or the contents therein, directly through our senses. Thus, we must infer the existence and characteristics of the mind in others, and in ourselves, based on repeated observations of others in relation to repeated observations of ourselves.

In common experience, intrinsic forms are considered to be "less real" or "unreal" in comparison to extrinsic forms, which are considered to be "more real" or simply "real" forms in comparison with their mental counterparts. Of course, both kinds of forms have reality, but it should be recognized that people tend to give ontological priority to their experience of extrinsic forms over that of intrinsic forms. However, it should also be recognized that many people experience forms that are considered to exist not only within themselves and their minds, but also internally beyond themselves and their minds.

A person's conscience is one such example. The experience of conscience and what it presents to one is clearly something that occurs within oneself, and yet, it may, at the same time, seem to be originating from beyond oneself. Conscience and other forms like it may be identified as *infra-intrinsic forms*, since they seem to arrive, in part, from the deeper recesses of our mind, and they may be considered as *super-intrinsic forms*, since they are experienced as above and beyond the human mind.

For most adult human beings, intrinsic forms are generally assumed to have subjective reality to the extent that they exist only within and by means of the minds of individuals, or groups of individuals. This seems true enough for many intrinsic forms, especially those of pure fantasy. However, this assumption does not hold true with certain other kinds of intrinsic forms such as that of mathematics. The equation 2+2=4, for example, exists as something true regardless of whether or not someone is aware of it, or whether or not someone understands it, or agrees with it, or feels good about it, etc. Some intrinsic forms, such as mathematical truths, could be considered as super-intrinsic as they seem to have objective reality that is independent of human understanding, though they may interact with human understanding as infra-intrinsic forms. Therefore, the subjectivity of intrinsic forms, though prevalent, is not absolute. Perhaps it is by approaching the mean between the extremes of the subjective and objective experiences of intrinsic forms that we may most accurately understand the reality of such forms.

Extrinsic forms, on the other hand, are generally assumed to have objective reality to the extent that they are considered to have existence that is independent of the human mind. It would not be consistent with common human experience to claim the opposite about extrinsic forms, namely, that the objective existence of any extrinsic form is, like many intrinsic forms, entirely dependent upon its perception such that it may exist only when it is perceived, viz., by an individual or group of individuals, and that it ceases to exist when it is not perceived. Certainly, this is not a practical outlook for human beings to maintain. Nevertheless, it is evident that the human mind is not entirely detached from its perceived extrinsic forms, since it is capable of knowing and influencing them to some degree. Furthermore, we have established earlier that the existence of consciousness is implied relative to the existence of every form, according to our definition of the term "form", and thereby consciousness is essentially inseparable from every form. Thus, as with intrinsic forms, it seems that it is through the approach of the mean between the extremes of the subjective and objective experience of extrinsic forms that the most commonsensical and accurate picture of that aspect of reality emerges.

3.1.2. LIMITATIONS

Form and the appearance of form can only be beheld and identified *as such* by a being with consciousness that is capable of holistic self-reflection. Through the self-reflecting consciousness, an individual may virtually detach from themselves and observe themselves as beholding things that are presented to them in unique ways relative to that of other things and the perspectives of other perceiving beings. Within our world, only *living* things born of the natural environment have true awareness, although some things that are contrived by conscious living beings may have a pseudo-awareness, as with advanced machines or robots. All living things, including human beings, have varying degrees of consciousness with the ability to behold forms and their unique appearances. Human beings, however, are the only known living creatures on earth with consciousness capable of holistic self-reflection, which enables them to not only behold any particular form and its appearance, but also to identify the essence of any particular form qua form with its appearance qua appearance.

Every living creature is able to apprehend forms with some degree of consciousness, but not every form can be apprehended by every living creature. Each living thing is unique in its abilities to perceive forms of different kinds. Many animals, for example, have senses that allow them to perceive extrinsic forms in their environment that other animals, including human beings, cannot perceive on their own. It seems that humans are the only living creatures that are able to contrive forms that can assist them in perceiving other forms which are beyond their natural capabilities of perception. Some common examples of this extension of human perception, which amounts to an extension of human consciousness, might be the invention of visual magnification devices such as the telescope or the microscope, each of which enable a human being to see the appearances of extrinsic forms that they could not otherwise see, or, at least, see well, with the naked eye.

With respect to intrinsic forms, it seems that human beings are the only creatures on earth capable of recognizing intrinsic forms as such. Although it appears that certain non-human animals do have the ability to perceive intrinsic forms within their minds, they do not appear to perceive themselves as having minds, which would enable them to identify their intrinsic forms as such. Furthermore, human beings are the only known living creatures on earth capable of thinking consciously and rationally about abstract intrinsic forms, such as beauty, truth, or goodness. Thus, human beings have a unique privilege, possessing not only the ability to holistically self-reflect, but also the ability to think about themselves in relation to their reality in both concrete and abstract terms.

While it is possible for certain intrinsic and extrinsic forms to be unknown to some or all living creatures with consciousness, it is not possible for any single form that exists to be wholly unknown or unknowable. Again, as we said earlier, the existence of consciousness is implied as a necessary constituent of the essence of every particular form. Even if there is a particular form that exists that is wholly unknown through the consciousness of every particular living creature, that particular form is necessarily knowable and known. How can this be? If every particular living creature with consciousness is unaware of some particular form, how can there be consciousness associated with that form? What is it that can know the existence of a form that escapes the consciousness of every particular living creature? That which knows the existence of every particular form, even as some forms may be unknown to some or all living creatures with consciousness, must, paradoxically, be something alive with consciousness that exists outside of the particularity of forms such that it cannot be categorized as something in particular or as a *finite* form. Anything that exists as finite can only exist as such *within* the totality of all that is finite; what is finite cannot transcend its finitude. This includes the consciousness of living creatures which renders them incapable of actually beholding the totality of finite things as something *other*.

Granted that every particular form that exists is in some way finite, viz., with limits and boundaries relative to that which it is *not*, the synthesis of every particular form must either be a particular form with boundaries, or it must be an infinite array of particular forms which does not have boundaries. If the synthesis of particular forms is an infinite array of particular forms, then the infinite array itself is what we might consider to be that which cannot be categorized as finite, as it is something boundless and beyond that of all particular forms, viz., the whole is greater than the sum of its parts. If, however, the synthesis of every particular form is a finite entity, then it is implied that something exists outside of its boundaries that is boundless. In this case, that which exists outside of the synthesis of all particular forms cannot logically be anything in particular for the reason that all particular forms must be encapsulated within the total synthesis of particular forms. Moreover, there can only be one thing that does not have boundaries, because if there were two or more things, these would be relative to themselves and they would implicitly have beginnings and ends to themselves in some essential way that would distinguish themselves from each other.

That which is capable of beholding the totality of particular things, whether it is an infinite array of particular things or something infinite relative to the finite totality of particular things, is something that must be truly and fully infinite such that it exists *within and beyond* the totality of finite things. This infinite reality cannot only exist outside of all finite things because this would render it as something finite with boundaries relative to all other finite things. The infinite reality must exist within and beyond all finite things to the extent that it unifies, encompasses, and comprises everything that exists. Thus, if every particular thing that exists within the totality of finite things is a particular form, and if each form is considered as a singular *being* that *is*, then what exists infinitely within and beyond the totality of finite things may be understood ontologically as absolute *Being*. In relation to particular *beings* as particular forms, we might also refer to absolute Being as absolute Form.

Once the existence of this absolute Being is concluded and properly understood, there are many implications about its nature that follow. One implication pertinent to our discussion is that absolute Being has consciousness, or, to put it more accurately, absolute Being is absolute Consciousness. As we have established that consciousness is a characteristic of living things, we might ask the question "What is the source of the consciousness of living things?". The answer to this question cannot finally rest in the particular living creatures relative to absolute Being. If absolute Being is the fullness of all that exists, which includes everything that has the potential to exist, how could it possibly lack something that only finite living creatures possess? The answer is that absolute Being, by definition, cannot be lacking in anything, and, therefore, absolute Being must serve implicitly as the living source of consciousness for all conscious creatures, without having a source for its own consciousness that is other than itself.

Consequently, if there is any particular form that is unknown to some or all living beings with consciousness, that which is unknown must certainly be knowable as it is known by absolute Being or absolute Form, which is absolute Consciousness. This absolute Consciousness is both an infra-intrinsic form that is treated as something particular within the human mind, and, ultimately, it is a super-intrinsic Form of all particular forms that must, by definition, be considered to exist not only within, but also beyond our finite minds.

3.2. CONSTITUTION

The *constitution* of any particular form, or that of which it consists is, first of all, aligned with our definition of "form" as something in particular that appears in a particular way. Any form's existence as something, together with its appearance, is what we would consider to be the form's fundamental constitution at the core of its essence. By extension, or logical implication, we may consider the constitution of any form in relation, not only to the category of constitution, but also to the categories of consciousness, potential, source, and function, as these are inseparable from the essence of any form. Of all things that contribute to the constitution of any form, it is a form's *appearance* that is the most apparent and pervasive.

3.2.1. APPEARANCE

The appearance of a form, which is, as we said, *how* a form is, must be accompanied by the existence of a form through consciousness, as something cannot appear to be in any way if it does not exist through consciousness; *that* something *is* must be ontologically concurrent with the way in which it appears to be by means of consciousness. Yet, it should be noted that the way in which something appears to be, which is inclusive of the categories of consciousness, constitution, potential, source, and function, is the evidence that something presents of its own existence. Without an appearance of some kind, a form cannot exist, nor can it be understood to exist by any consciousness; a form without an appearance is inconceivable nonsense. Therefore, something must exist in order for it to have an appearance, but the appearance of something is essential to the existence of something; the true appearance of any form is an integral part of the essence of any form.

The appearance of any finite thing as form can always be transcended, as that which is finite, by definition, must have limits, which logically implies something that exists beyond itself and its appearance. Transcendence of the appearance of any given thing can happen either by apprehending the boundaries of the thing holistically in relation to anything which exists outside of itself that it is *not*, or by examining any individual aspect of the appearance of the thing. With respect to the latter, when a part that contributes to the whole of a form's appearance is observed as an object in its own right, and even when a part of a part of the whole of a form's appearance is objectified, the overarching form's appearance is effectively transcended to and through its objectified part. Moreover, the objectified part of the whole is also transcended through the apprehension if its boundaries relative to the surrounding whole in which it participates.

Thus, we may affirm that 1.) the appearance of every particular form is always *internal* to that of something other than itself such that it is seated within a finite or infinite succession of the appearances of forms, or otherwise it is a final appearance of a final form, which is the finite synthesis of all finite forms and their appearances, relative to something outside of itself that isn't finite, and 2.) the appearance of every form is *external* to something that lies within or beneath it, which, in turn, presents an appearance that can be transcended to reveal something within or beneath it, and so on, ad infinitum. Regarding the latter conclusion, let us observe that as the appearance of every form consists of the appearance of other forms, there must be an infinite regress of the appearances of forms without any impenetrable and final finite substance, even if the appearance of a particular form consists of the appearance of forms of the same kind, which, in turn, consist of the appearance of forms of the same kind, and so on, ad infinitum. The appearance of every form consists of the appearance of forms to infinite regress because it is logically impossible for the division or analysis of the appearance of any form, which reveals its consistency, to end, just as it is logically impossible to continuously divide and subdivide any linear distance to arrive at a final length.

The infinite regress of the appearance of forms that results from analyzing the consistency of the appearance of forms is itself greater than the sum of its parts. This infinite regress is both immanent and transcendent with respect to the finite appearances of finite forms, and to this extent we may identify it as the absolute Appearance of absolute Form. Similarly, the infinite succession of the appearance of forms within the appearance of forms is itself greater than the sum of its parts and exists within and beyond the finite appearances of finite forms. This infinite succession is the same as that which exists outside of the finite synthesis of every finite appearance of every finite form, which may be identified as the absolute Appearance of absolute Form. Therefore, at the extreme of the regressive division of the appearances of forms, and at the extreme of the successive synthesis of the appearances of forms, we find an infinite and absolute One, that, ontologically, is absolute Being as absolute Appearance of absolute Form, which unifies, encompasses, and comprises everything that exists. If we grant that this is the case, then we must acknowledge that reality is ontologically hierarchical such that everything in particular extends from and moves toward the absolute.

3.2.1.1. BOUNDARIES

Boundaries are essential to the existence and apprehension of every form through their appearance, that is, in the sense that we are using the term "form". The boundaries of the appearance of a given form contribute to the differentiation of the form from other forms and enable us to apprehend the form as a singular entity, which we might refer to, basically, as a 'this' or a set of 'these' relative to a 'that' or a set of 'those'. When the appearance of any form is encountered, its boundaries are always in relation to something other than itself, which can include the person that encounters the form, insofar as a difference between the form and that which is other than the form is apparent through their juxtaposition; a particular form is never found to exist in isolation, but rather it is at all times finite in relation to something other than itself. This fact is not only experiential, but it is also a quantitative rule as the singularity of any entity always logically implies plurality, viz., one implies another; the awareness of "this" implies a differentiation between "this" and some "that" which is *not* "this".

Often the boundaries of the appearances of forms are experienced as clear and distinct in relation to other forms. However, it should be observed that sometimes the boundaries of the appearances of forms are not hard lined, but conceptually *implied* by the arrangement of multiple forms. A picket fence that encloses a yard is one example which demonstrates implied boundaries. In this case, we may consider the yard with its space to be contained by the fence even though the forms of the fence assembly are limited in their material extension and they are spaced apart from each other horizontally at regular intervals with their lowest point near or in direct contact with the yard. This situation creates a sense of enclosure to some degree, yet the yard is not entirely enclosed by the fence.

Sometimes the boundaries of the appearances of forms are ostensible, but not easy to define clearly. For example, when the colors of the visible spectrum are perceived, the differentiation between adjacent colors is obvious although it is not clear as to where, precisely, the boundaries between adjacent colors are located. In this case, definitive boundaries must be artificially imposed in thought or through a representation of the experience.

One may also become aware that the boundaries of the appearance of a given form, once perceived as clear and distinct, become increasingly unclear and indistinct when they are examined at different scales. A generalized example of this would be when an edge of a physical object is magnified for visual examination. Without the memory of what is under examination, it may be difficult to know what it is that is under examination.

As we said, the boundaries of the appearances of particular forms are always relative to that which is other than themselves. However, the set of all particular forms, which is the combination of all particular forms into one particular form, must have boundaries relative not only to the particular forms that participate in its totality, but also to what exists outside of its boundaries which cannot be any particular form with an appearance that has boundaries. That which is without form is necessarily without appearance and without boundaries; what is formless and invisible, with respect to appearance, is limitless. Thus, the synthesis of all particular forms as something in particular must be seated in, and surrounded by, something that is nothing in particular and infinitely formless. As a matter of logic, any particular form, as such, can only be understood in light of what is formless, and the collective boundaries of all particular forms are only apprehended by means of the boundless.

There are some particular things that we might experience which can appear to be formless from certain perspectives, although these particular things cannot be formless, ultimately. In such cases, it may be difficult to discern the exact location of boundaries, so to speak, yet it is at least possible to apprehend that boundaries exist.

The everyday experience of *water* is one example of a substance that does not seem have any particular form that is inherent or fixed. Although the average experience of water gives evidence to the boundaries of water, these boundaries depend on the boundaries of other forms and the way in which these other forms act upon the water; water, as it is commonly experienced, does not appear to have a form of its own except in connection with the form of its container and that of which the water might contain. Thus, without the boundaries of other particular forms, water tends toward formlessness and scatters. Moreover, when contained water contains other forms within itself, it may have an apparent formlessness relative to the forms that it contains such that it serves as a supportive setting for the existence of the contained forms which allows the boundaries of the contained forms to be perceived in the foreground. The essential contrast between the water and its container, as well as the essential contrast between what the water contains, may give rise to the awareness of the water as having boundaries with respect to its identity in the sense that it is *not* what contains it, nor what it contains.

Another example of something that tends toward formlessness is the *sky*, or earth's atmosphere, as perceived from the vantage point of a person grounded on earth. From this perspective, it may appear that the sky is something formless, as its vast expanse contains, and contrasts with, other particular forms that may have clear and distinct boundaries. Yet, from a vantage point outside of the earth, the sky has boundaries that depend upon the extent of it, as the earth's atmosphere, from the earth into the space that surrounds it. The boundaries of the appearances of particular forms that are perceived on earth simultaneous with the sky, such as that of the moon, the stars, cumulus clouds, rain drops, etc., become apparent by means of the enveloping and seemingly formless nature of the sky from that point of view. Without the apparent boundaries of the objects in the sky relative to the apparent boundlessness of the sky, there would not be a noticeable difference between the objects and the sky in the measure that each is apprehended as *not* the other. Likewise, without the apparent boundaries of the sky relative to the space that surrounds it, there would not be any perceivable difference between the sky and its spatial container.

Yet another example of something that could be considered formless, which is present in the previous two examples and seemingly closer to true formlessness, is the physical *space* that exists both within and outside of a person's body. Like water and the earth's atmosphere, physical spaces have boundaries that are derived from the forms that contain them as well as the forms that they might contain. Particular spaces can have a formless quality if they bring other forms to the forefront while remaining in the background, although these particular spaces could also appear to have form due to the supportive boundaries of the forms which contain and submissively highlight them. The aggregate of all particular spaces, which we might call 'Space', does not yield a final spatial form with definitive spatial boundaries that encloses and includes all particular spaces, unless what is considered to be outside of the boundaries of Space is not Space, not spatial, and not treated spatially; if Space is considered to be a final spatial form with spatial boundaries that consists of all particular spaces with spatial boundaries, what could be outside of those boundaries but more space, unless that which is considered to be beyond the boundaries of Space is something other than Space and understood according to different terms?; Space, as the set of all particular spaces, is inconceivable as a final spatial form in relation to itself, although it may be understood as *something in particular in relation to what is not Space, which includes* every other particular form.

Relative to space, and similar to space as an example of something that can appear to be formless with a tendency toward true formlessness, is *time*. Immediate instances, or moments, of time are bound by their duration, viz., their location in the "here" and "now", so to speak, which is understood relative to other durations consisting of both past and future time in which such instances implicitly participate. These other durations of time, in turn, necessarily participate in, and are bound by, even more durations of time outside of themselves toward a seemingly infinite duration of time. The aggregate of all particular moments in time, which we might call 'Time', cannot logically be contained within the boundaries of duration as a final temporal form since its boundaries would imply that there is a particular time before and after the duration, unless what is considered to be outside of the boundaries of Time is not Time and not treated in terms of time. Like Space, Time, as the set of all particular moments of time, is inconceivable as an all-inclusive form in relation to itself, although it may be understood as something in particular in relation to what is not Time, which includes every other particular form.

Despite the fact that there are some particular things in our experience that may seem to be formless or resemble formlessness, such as water, sky, space, and time, only that which is not something in particular relative to other particular things can be truly formless. Every form, according to our initial definition of the term, must be something in particular with distinct appearances in relation to that which they are not. Therefore, something formless cannot be something in particular with a particular appearance.

What is formless such that it cannot be something in particular and its non-particularity is invisible, or without a distinct appearance? The answer to this question must be something that exists infinitely outside of the boundaries of the aggregate of all particular things such that there is no exterior limit to itself. At the same time, it must exist infinitely within the boundaries of all particular things lest it be bounded and excluded by the boundaries of the aggregate of all particular things as well as the boundaries of the particular things which participate in the aggregate of all particular things. Thus, what is truly formless must be infinitely transcendent and imminent with respect to every particular thing.

Paradoxically, the only something in particular that is ultimately a formless and invisible nothing in particular is *Being*, which is, as we mentioned before, the totality of all particular forms as particular beings. As the totality of all particular beings that exist, any supposed location "outside" of the ontological boundaries of Being, so to speak, is inconceivable, that is, in terms of existence, because anything that is thought to exist "outside" of the boundaries of Being, which might be considered as *other* than Being or as *not* Being, must have existence of some kind. Of course, any particular being may be treated as other than Being, or as not Being, in the sense that it is not the totality of Being, and Being may be treated as other than, or as not, any particular being since it is not a particular being. Nevertheless, it should be observed that the otherness and ontological negation between Being and particular beings is not a relationship between equal finite items or entities. Rather the finite existence of every particular being is subordinate to the infinite existence of Being in a hierarchical manner such that Being is greater than the sum of the particular beings that participate in its ontological essence. Every particular thing, which includes every particular human person, is a bounded form that is fundamentally a singular being that has existence derived from Being. Though we may treat Being as if it is something in particular, that is, as a finite form which stands relative to other particular things and in subordination to our scrutiny, we are incapable of fully objectifying Being, as it must, by definition, extend infinitely within and beyond our physical and psychological boundaries.

Being contains all forms and it is contained within all forms to the extent of the boundaries of those forms. As the fullness of everything that *is*, Being must be a singular entity that does not have boundaries outside of itself. However, when Being is considered as a singular reality, viz., as a "this" or "that", the existence of plurality is logically implied, which can only be found *within* the essence of Being, that is, in relation to the particular beings that necessarily participate in the essence of Being; the oneness of the essence of Being pervades and unifies the multiplicity of essences that correspond to every particular being; the existence of Being implies the existence of that which is *not* Being, which can only have a finite existence as *a* being within the totality of Being. Our previous examples of water, sky, space, and time, as seemingly formless things, are particular beings which are *not* Being that participate in the essence of Being. Even the absolutization of Space and Time should be considered as *not* Being with respect to their particular categories of existence, although because these are boundless and formless within themselves, they may be understood as absolute expressions or *modes* of Being.

Although Being is truly formless and invisible due to its infinite ontological infiltration of, and expansion beyond, all boundaries, Being does have the semblance of a bounded form with an "appearance" in relation to its essence that can be understood by means of that which Being is *not*. As we said earlier, Being is absolute Appearance which relates to all particular appearances. As such, we might say that Being emanates itself from itself toward particular forms within itself, while the relative appearances of all particular forms subsist in Being and emanate toward each other and ultimately toward Being as absolute Appearance. Furthermore, Being as Appearance is the same as Consciousness, which beholds the totality of every particular being, including those beings with limited consciousness. Yet, a particular being with limited consciousness cannot possibly behold the totality of Being as absolute Appearance, as absolute Consciousness. Therefore, any "appearance" of Being is as limited as the consciousness of any particular being that beholds it.

Beyond our sense of the "appearance" of Being as a formless and boundaryless existence relative to that of other particular beings which exist within Being, there are many other things that we might identify as the "appearance" of the nature of Being, among the most significant of which are the various modes of Being mentioned above. Of these modes, absolute *Quantity* is an important expression of the boundaries of the "appearance" of Being with respect to its unification of many particular beings within itself as one Being. Accordingly, we might observe that within the oneness of Being, which unites the many particular beings, there is an overarching logical structure that is fundamentally *triune*. This structure becomes evident when we realize that the existence of Being implies the existence of non-Being, which necessitates the existence of a third unifying element as the synthesis of Being and non-Being. The synthesis of Being and non-Being also *implies the existence of an antithesis in relation to itself, which neces*-sitates the existence of a third unifying element as the synthesis of the synthesis of Being and non-Being with the antithesis of the synthesis of Being and non-Being, and so on, ad infinitum. This infinite trinitarian relationship within Being is found to occur in a fractal manner with respect to the relationship between individual beings that exist within the infinite boundaries of Being.

Any consciousness that is aware of itself in a holistic way such as that of human beings, which is an essential feature that differentiates human beings from all other animals, is a central ingredient to *personhood*. Since the nature of consciousness is such that it always requires an object of which it is aware, and because there is no object that can exist as essentially *other* than absolute Consciousness in the sense that it exists *outside* of its boundaries, the object of the awareness of absolute Consciousness must be that of itself in relation to its particular constituents. This, of course, implies that absolute Consciousness is absolute Personhood, which must serve as the source of all particular manifestations of personhood. Moreover, because human beings are the only known bearers, among particular forms, of the character trait that is personhood through the self-reflective brand of consciousness, human beings necessarily resemble and share the awareness of absolute Consciousness to some extent. In this sense, any given human being, as a living form, is an *incarnation* of absolute Consciousness to some degree. Certainly, the highest degree and extreme expression of incarnation is possible among human beings, which would be the architype of every other incarnation as the fullness of absolute Consciousness embodied in human form. Note that we may come to conclude *what it is like* for Being to exist as absolute Consciousness in relation to itself and every particular form through our participation in absolute Consciousness as we know *what it is* to exist in relation to ourselves and the appearance of the particular forms that exist within and beyond ourselves.

3.2.1.2. CONTENTS

If the appearance of every particular form has boundaries, then it is logically implied that the appearance of every particular form has *contents* within its boundaries which stands in relation to its boundaries and what is outside of its boundaries. The contents of the appearance of any form contribute to its manifestation and differentiation among other forms. Note that the appearances of intrinsic and extrinsic forms cannot be void of contents. If someone considers the appearance of something to be an extrinsic form, but it is found by others to be imperceptible to the senses and void of extrinsic content, then the appearance is not a proper extrinsic form, but rather it is an intrinsic form that is perceptible by the mind, and, as such, it cannot be void of content.

Although the contents of forms may vary greatly, and this variance gives rise to the many different appearances of forms which are separated by their boundaries, every particular form can be categorized by the uniqueness of the contents of its appearance in relation to other forms that either do or do not have the same contents in common. One general example of how we might categorize forms is in terms of the way in which their contents are structured, or organized, both by means of their boundaries and as participants in the existence of their boundaries. Let us consider the intrinsic form of a *square* as a specific example of this kind of categorization. A square has two parallel sides of equal length that are separated to the extent of the perpendicular lengths of two other parallel sides which are separated to the extent of the perpendicular lengths of the former sides. In this geometry, each side is connected at its ends with two other sides perpendicular to it, which generates a form with four right angles in respective quadrants. The square form is an organization of four, straight, one-dimensional lines of equal length as two perpendicular pairs that are symmetrical about a central point. The space enclosed by the square form is the essential content of the form that exists in relation to the form's boundaries, and the boundaries of the form, in turn, exist in relation to the space that they enclose. Other forms with this same fundamental organization, or, at least, with an organization that tends toward this end, may be categorized as square-shaped forms. Such forms may differ in material, size, weight, surface pattern, texture, etc., but all of them can be grouped within a square category as they share the same, or similar, overall organization of contents in relation to their boundaries.

There is always some kind of space, so to speak, that surrounds and pervades the boundaries of the appearances of particular forms, yet the differentiation of forms through their boundaries does not necessarily imply that the forms are separated in this space with respect to a specific essence, although they may be. Often the boundaries of a particular form are *nested* within the space of the boundaries of another form, which, in turn, may have boundaries that are nested within the space of the boundaries of another form, and so on. Some of the boundaries of nested forms may even be shared with the boundaries of the form within which they occur. In any case, forms may exist within forms at different scales.

The appearance of a singular form that is observed to have other forms participating in its appearance, at a lesser scale, within its boundaries might be called the "master" appearance, or "master" form, in relation to its contents, each of which we might call the "subordinate" appearance, or "subordinate" form. This is basically a part-to-whole relationship. Absolute Consciousness, Space, and Time, mentioned earlier, are among the most extreme examples of master forms in relation to their participating subordinate forms, and each of these master forms with their subordinate forms participate, ultimately as subordinate forms, in absolute Being as the absolute master Form.

Accordingly, all subordinate forms may be treated as attributes of their master form. These attributes are what the form is made of, so to speak, and they participate in its expression. Some of these attributes may be crucial to the existence of the form to which they belong such that if they were to be removed from their master form, or modified in some way, the essence of the master form would be changed. Each master form or subordinate form may be regarded as a *unit* in the sense that it is complete within itself when considered in relation to other units. Any master form or subordinate form may be apprehended as either an individual unit or as set of units, which are treated as external in some way to the person that encounters them. Additionally, it is worth noting that anything which serves as a master form is an attribute of itself, as one may refer to the form *of* this or that. Thus, a master form *is* a form, which *has* a form that is inclusive of subordinate forms. Of course, Being as the master Form of all forms can be considered in this manner, however it should be recognized that its ultimate essence is not only immanent with respect to all particular forms, but it is also absolutely transcendent with respect to particular forms such that it cannot be transcended and found to exist within any other master form.

A four-legged table assembly is one example of a particular master form that consists of a basic set of units, namely, four legs and a table-top, each of which serve as unitary subordinate forms within the boundaries of the table. In this primarily visual and tactile example, if the physicality of the table assembly as the master form is emphasized holistically when perceived by the senses, that is to say, not in terms of an assembly, but as a tangible monolith that is indivisible and uniform, then the subordinate forms which participate in the master form may be abstracted as ideas through analysis. If, however, the assemblance or the physical reality of the parts of the master form are emphasized over and above the physical reality of the master form, then the master form is an idea in which the subordinate forms, that are perceived by the senses, participate. In this latter case, our table assembly is experienced as a physical reality, but it is understood *conceptually*, while the subordinate forms of the table assembly that are perceived by the senses, are juxtaposed physical objects which serve as essential parts of the whole table assembly concept.

In the preceding example, the four-legged table was determined at the outset to be an assembly, and so we had clear knowledge of it as such. In experience, however, it is possible for one to consider a particular master form as monolithic, and it is also possible for one to consider a master form to be an assembly that otherwise might be considered as monolithic. Let us note that if the actual parts of what is considered to be an assembled master form, or the abstracted parts of what is considered to be a monolithic master form, are examined more closely, as if separated from their master form, they may be found to have subordinate forms, which would render them as a master forms relative to their parts. This suggests that our perception of something as monolithic could be illusory. In fact, every human-made object is a kind of assembly, and we would be hard pressed to find any object in nature that does not have component parts. Therefore, it seems that virtually every appearance of every particular form, by way of its boundaries as a master form in concert with the boundaries of its subordinate forms, is an assembly of some kind with part-to-whole relationships.

The contents within the boundaries of the appearances of extrinsic forms have actual volume, as extrinsic forms exist in physical space with spatial locations relative to their boundaries. By contrast, the contents within the boundaries of the appearances of intrinsic forms are ostensible, as intrinsic forms do not exist in physical space with actual spatial locations relative to their boundaries. In this regard, all intrinsic forms could be considered as two-dimensional since they do not have actual spatial depth.

The appearances of intrinsic and extrinsic forms always have contents that are essential to their existence, and these forms may also be associated with contents that are non-essential to their existence; it is impossible for intrinsic and extrinsic forms to exist with a bounded appearance that is without essential contents, while it is possible for such forms to be, or not be, associated with non-essential contents. Every instance of essential contents is ultimately a form with an appearance that consists of essential contents, which may or may not include non-essential contents, and these essential contents, in turn, consist of essential contents, which may or may not include non-essential contents, and so on, ad infinitum. Likewise, it is possible for the appearance of a form with essential contents to be found as part of the essential contents of the appearance of another form of a larger scale, which, in turn, may be found to be part of the essential contents of the appearance of another form of an even larger scale, and so on. Thus, it seems that we may have essential contents, and potentially non-essential contents, within the appearance of forms at smaller and larger scales.

Non-essential contents of any given form always share the boundaries of the appearance of that form in some way and to some extent. However, non-essential contents do not contribute to, or participate in, the existence of the boundaries of the appearance of any established form within which they reside. If the non-essential contents of the appearance of a given form were to be removed from the appearance of the form, their absence would not compromise the boundaries and existence of the appearance of the form with respect to what it has been established to be in essence.

Of course, it is also possible for the appearance of a form to have essential contents, which participate in its boundaries, while having non-essential contents that exist independently both within the boundaries of the appearance of the form and beyond the boundaries of the essential contents that give the form its definition. One general example of the latter, which is primarily visual and tactile, is an object in a container of some sort. In this case, the object is a form with an appearance that exists within the form of the container, but it exists independently of the boundaries of the appearance of the container. If the container of the object is transparent to some degree, and if the object that it contains is relatively opaque with differences in comparison to the container, then the appearance of the container and the object will likely manifest as distinct entities, or otherwise their appearances will coincide and be perceived as if they were a unified appearance of only one thing. Similarly, if the container of the object is opaque and semi-enclosed such that it affords a view to the object that it contains, and if the object that it contains is also relatively opaque with differences in comparison to the container, then the appearance of the container and the object will likely manifest as distinct entities, or otherwise their appearances will coincide and be perceived as if they were a unified appearance of only one thing. If, however, the container of the object is either transparent or opaque, while the object that it contains is either transparent or opaque such that its appearance matches that of its container, then the apparent distinction between the appearance of the object and that of its container will be minimal to none.

Moreover, non-essential contents are ultimately forms with appearances that consist of essential contents that are non-essential relative to the essential contents of their master form, which may have non-essential contents within their boundaries, which, in turn, consist of essential contents, again non-essential relative to the essential contents of the original master form, that may have non-essential contents within their boundaries, and so on, ad infinitum. Likewise, it is possible for a form with essential contents to be found as non-essential content within another form of a larger scale, which, in turn, may be found to be non-essential content within another form of a larger scale, and so on. Thus, it seems that we may have non-essential contents within the essential contents of master forms at smaller and larger scales.

Note that the boundaries of a form do not determine the contents of the form, but rather the essential contents of a form determine the boundaries of the form; the essential contents of a form are always ontologically prior to, and co-dependent with, the boundaries of a form; the boundaries of any form, though they are united to the form's essential contents, are always subordinate to, and abstracted from, the essential contents of any form. Even in the case of implied boundaries which suggest the existence of a form, there are essential contents which contribute to the implication of the form. However, the essential contents of any particular extrinsic or intrinsic form participate in the boundaries of the form in combination with that which is *outside* of the boundaries of the form. In other words, the essential contents of the form and that which is *not* the form contributes to the existence of the boundaries of the form. A cumulus cloud is one of many examples of an extrinsic form with essential contents that determine its boundaries, which are the apparent edges of the cloud against the background of the sky, as perceived from a distance on the ground. In this example, it seems obvious that the cumulus cloud has boundaries that cannot be disconnected from its contents, nor can its boundaries be taken out of relation with that which exists outside of them. The removal of the contents at the apparent edges of the cumulus cloud in relation to the surrounding sky would terminate the existence of the cloud in actual space.

Although it may seem possible for a form and its boundaries to entirely lack contents, as with a hollowed object, that which creates the boundaries of the form serves as the essential contents of the form, while the emptiness within the form that is perceived to exist beyond the essential contents is non-essential to the degree that it can be filled without compromising the boundaries of the form. In another sense, however, any void within the boundaries of a form contributes to the inner boundaries of the essential contents as that which the essential contents are *not*, while the outer boundaries of the essential contents that comprise the form are also defined by that which the essential contents of the form are *not*.

If we were to be presented with any natural or unnatural form, and if we were to begin to subtract from the form its contents, at what point in the process of subtraction would the essence of the form cease to be? Whether we are considering a form that is perceived through our senses or a form that is perceived psychologically, or if we are considering a form that is perceived both through our senses and psychologically to some degree, the existence of any form is dependent upon the essential aspects of what is understood to be its given form. For example, if we consider a triangle with blue sides as the given form, and if we were to subtract the blue color from the sides of the triangle, we would not be able to subtract the color without also subtracting the sides of the triangle, which would negate the triangle altogether. If the triangular form with its blue colored sides were to be perceived as given in relation to a background of any color or absence of color other than the blue color of the sides of the triangle, how would the sides be perceived if the blue color was removed and not replaced with some other perceivable color or linear absence of color that contrasts with that of its background? Thus, in this case, the blue color of the sides of the triangle in relation to the background of the triangle is essential to the given triangular form. If, alternatively, we were to consider a triangle with blue sides, but we determined that the triangle was the given form, which also happened to have blue sides as non-essential contents, then subtracting and replacing the color of the sides would be inconsequential to the existence of the given triangular form. In this case, the subtraction of even one side of the triangle would obliterate its essence as a triangle, which, simultaneously, would obliterate the coincidental and subordinate color of the side that was removed.

Undoing the essence of a form by removing the necessary constituents of its constitution also involves the removal or alteration of the particular consciousness, potential, source, and function associated with the form. If, to use a previous example related to the function of a form, we subtract the tabletop of a four-legged table, the table ceases to be as such and cannot be used for its usual purpose, namely, to support and organize objects in order to facilitate human activity in relation to said objects. In this case, the tabletop is a necessary aspect of the table as it is the essential content that participates in the boundaries of its appearance, which includes that of its function. If, however, we were to subtract limited portions of contents from the tabletop by poking many small holes in it while leaving the overall structure of the tabletop intact, we would have changed the appearance of the table, and perhaps affected its performance to some degree, but its essence and function as a table would remain. Let us observe that it is possible to destroy the essence of a particular form, while suggesting the *idea* of the same essence. If we consider a four-legged table and remove all of the tabletop material except a certain thickness of its perimeter, the table will not qualify as a functional table, although it may be suggestive of one. If we take a triangle and add small, closely spaced, gaps in each of its three sides, the triangle will then cease to be a triangle, but the resulting juxtaposition of forms point to the idea of a triangle through implication.

3.2.1.3. DIMENSIONS

We might refer to the extent of the appearances of any particular form, both intrinsic and extrinsic, as "dimensions". Although the term "dimensions" is usually associated with the linear extension of extrinsic forms as perceived by our senses of sight, touch, and, to some degree, sound, which, as we said, are the predominant senses associated with the common use of the word "form", the term "dimensions" may also be applied metaphorically to every intrinsic and extrinsic form, according to our use of the term "form", to indicate the various ways in which the boundaries of the appearances of forms through their contents are manifested. Of course, these dimensions are, themselves, not found to be disassociated from the appearance of any form; dimensions cannot be understood except in a subordinate relationship to a form that has them. Moreover, dimensions are not entities that are found to occupy physical space as extrinsic forms are found to do, however, dimensions are considered through experience as participatory aspects of perceived forms, both intrinsic and extrinsic, such that this or that object *has* certain dimensions. Therefore, it appears that dimensions are ultimately intrinsic forms that are abstracted from intrinsic and extrinsic forms.

The extent of the appearances of extrinsic forms to their boundaries can often be quantified through units of *measurement* that correspond to the particular dimension of appearance under consideration. For example, we might consider the temperature, weight, length, intensity of the sound, etc., of a given extrinsic form using units of measurement that are suited for each category. Unless intrinsic forms are represented with physical means that can be measured, or an arbitrarily imagined standard of measurement is applied to intrinsic forms that are considered to have unalterable characteristics relative to each other, the extent of the appearances of intrinsic forms are not measurable from the perspective of the subject that beholds them as such. Nevertheless, it seems possible that the boundaries of the appearances of intrinsic forms could be determined through measurement in some way by someone other than the subject if the other person were to somehow gain experiential access to those forms as extrinsic to themselves.

Let us examine the literal dimensions of extrinsic forms, viz., according to the usual application of the term "dimensions", as examples that may be representative of the other kinds of "dimensions", which serve as measurable aspects of extrinsic forms. When extrinsic forms are perceived through the senses of sight, touch, and sound, they are often experienced as *three-dimensional* with respect to their linear extension. Extrinsic forms that involve the senses of sight, touch, and sound are always *actually* three-dimensional, while intrinsic forms that reflect the same senses are *ostensibly* three-dimensional. An extrinsic form, as actually three-dimensional, has *volume*, which is the amount of space that the form occupies or encloses. An intrinsic form may be apparently three-dimensional, in which case it would have an apparent volume. Actual and apparent three-dimensional forms consist of two, one, and zero-dimensional forms which contribute to their actual or apparent volume. The actual volume of any actual three-dimensional form is fundamentally comprised of height, width, and depth. *Height* may be defined as a vertical measurement, relative to width and depth, which encapsulates the maximum linear expanse of something from its base to its top, or from its top to its base. *Width* may be defined as a horizontal measurement, relative to height and depth, which encapsulates the maximum linear expanse of something from one of its sides to another. *Depth* may be defined as the horizontal measurement, relative to height and width, which encapsulates the maximum linear expanse of something from its front to its back, or from its back to its front.

Note that the actual volume, height, width, and depth of an actual three-dimensional form are themselves intrinsic forms that are abstracted attributes of the actual three-dimensional form as perceived by the senses. Although the apparent volume of any intrinsic form that is apparently three-dimensional may also have an apparent height, width, and depth, these apparent aspects of the apparent three-dimensional form cannot be measured apart from physical associations or a fixed standard for comparison. Any extrinsic form that is a two-dimensional representation of a three-dimensional form, such as a rendering of a cube on a relatively flat medium, consists of actual three-dimensional forms with actual height, width, and depth due to the physical nature of the materials that were used to create it. Three-dimensional forms can be experienced *explicitly*, viz., unbroken in height, width, and depth, or they may be experienced *implicitly* by the arrangement of at least four points, which may consist of at least four other forms at four points, in relative proximity, that generate a sense of linear height, width, and depth. Explicit and implicit three-dimensional forms can also be configured to participate in the implication of other dimensional forms of a larger scale.

A *two-dimensional* form, as compared to a three-dimensional form, is a *plane*, which is an extruded line or extruded set of lines, that is characterized as having only height and width; two-dimensional forms are completely flat, lacking entirely in the depth which enables volume. Two-dimensional forms are not found in the physical environment as extrinsic forms. Rather, they may be abstracted from both intrinsic and extrinsic forms through analytical reasoning. Thus, a two-dimensional form could be considered as a property of some actual or apparent two or three-dimensional form that one might experience. Any extrinsic form that is a two-dimensional representation of a two-dimensional form, such as a rendering of a square plane on a relatively flat medium, consists of actual three-dimensional forms with actual height, width, and depth due to the physical nature of the materials that were used to create it. In this case, the representation of the square plane could be measured in some way using standard units of measurement, however, without an association to something physical or a fixed standard for comparison, the square plane, as an intrinsic form, cannot be measured. As with three-dimensional forms, two-dimensional forms can be experienced *explicitly*, viz., unbroken in height and width, or they may be experienced *implicitly* by the arrangement of at least three points, which may consist of at least three other forms at three points, in relative proximity, that generate a sense of linear height and width. Explicit and implicit two-dimensional forms can also be configured to participate in the implication of other dimensional forms of a larger scale.

A *one-dimensional* form is a *line*, which is an extruded point with the qualities of location and extension relative to that of another form. Like two-dimensional forms, one-dimensional forms do not exist as extrinsic forms. Rather, they are intrinsic forms that may be abstracted from both intrinsic and extrinsic forms through analytic reasoning. Thus, a one-dimensional form could be considered as a property of some actual or apparent one, two, or three-dimensional form that a person might experience. A line, in theory, does not have any height, width, or depth unless it is oriented and compared to another form according to these categories. For example, a line segment may be oriented vertically and compared to another line segment or other object with respect to its height. If a line is represented though a particular medium in physical space, it will consist of actual three-dimensional forms which can be measured with standard units of measurement. As with two and three-dimensional forms, one-dimensional lines can be experienced *explicitly*, viz., unbroken in extension, or they can be experienced *implicitly* by at least two points, which may consist of at least two other forms at two points, in relative proximity, that generate a sense of linear extension. Explicit and implied one-dimensional lines can also be configured to participate in the implication of other dimensional forms of a larger scale.

A *zero-dimensional* form is a non-dimensional *point* that may locate, or be abstracted from, any intrinsic or extrinsic form associated with our dominant senses. A point is non-dimensional because it may only be described theoretically in terms of its location relative to other locations in space, as it does not have any height, width, or depth. However, if a theoretical point is represented through some medium in physical space, it will consist of actual three-dimensional forms which can be measured with standard units of measurement. If a point is grouped with other points in an organized set such that another form is *implied*, as with the three vertices of a triangle for example or the various constellations which may appear as points in the night sky, the implied form made possible by the set of points is zero-dimensional with respect to physical space, although other dimensions may apply in a mental space. Points as zero-dimensional forms are foundational to all other types of dimensional forms, as a point can be abstracted from, and utilized to construct, virtually any part of a one, two, or three-dimensional form.

3.2.1.4. INTEGRITY

Of course, we should acknowledge that any appearance that has been identified as such tends to suggest the possibility of something behind the appearance that is either *consistent* or *inconsistent* with the essence of the appearance; when we say that something "appears to be the case", we subjectify our view of whatever it is that we are observing and leave room for the possibility that what "appears to be the case" for us either *is* what it appears to be, or it is *not* what it appears to be. We might refer to the former as a "true" appearance, and we might refer to the latter as a "false" appearance in relation to the degree to which the appearance of the underlying form, or form group, *participates* in the essence of the appearance as contents. Note that if an appearance is inconsistent with an underlying form, acting as a *mask* that conceals the underlying form, the appearance is at least consistent with itself and the essence of the appearance of its own form.

A person who intentionally wears a costume that appears to be different than the normal or natural appearance of the person is one obvious example of a false appearance. In this case, the person wearing the costume does not want the appearance of the costume to match that of their normal or natural appearance. Let us note that with the term "costume" we are not simply referring to the wearing of clothes, although clothes are examples of forms with appearances that suggest and conceal underlying forms to some degree. Rather, with this example, we are talking about any personal garment, adornment, or the like that is not usually worn by, or expected to be worn by, a particular person. In that sense of the word, it seems reasonable to conclude that a person wearing a costume would only choose to do so for a preferred *audience*, which may include, or be exclusively, themselves.

From the perspective of the audience of the person wearing a costume, it's possible that there is initially no distinction between the costume and its wearer, such that the audience is fooled into believing that the costume is not a costume, but the normal or natural appearance of the person wearing the costume. This situation may also be accompanied with specific behaviors that are not normal or natural to the person wearing the costume with the possible effect of further convincing the audience that the person is the same as what or who they appear to be. Otherwise, from the perspective of the audience of the person wearing the costume, it is possible that there is some perceived degree of distinction between the costume and its wearer. In this situation, the costume wearer may not be attempting to completely fool their audience, but rather to entertain them, as with the actors in a play, or to invite them to deny, at least temporarily, that they are aware of any other appearance that is more authentic than what is being presented.

Alternatively, the costume wearer may be attempting to completely fool their audience for some purpose, however, they are failing to do so.

Note that if the costume wearer initially shocks or surprises their audience with their costume, the audience must have been aware of the normal or natural appearance of the person, and/or the audience had an expectation of what the person should be wearing in the given circumstance, prior to the wearing of the costume. Although the audience in this case has knowledge that the appearance of the costume wearer is not consistent with their normal or natural appearance, and/or with the expectation of the given circumstance, if the charade persists long enough, viz., over an extended period of time, the audience is more likely to begin to accept that the costume is part of the person's normal or natural appearance and the audience may even become fully convinced that the costume is not a costume, however inappropriate it may be for the given circumstance.

Another related example of a false appearance that we might consider, though it is not usually considered as such, is that of representational art. Similar to the costume, which can be a kind of representational art in relation to its wearer, there are degrees of accuracy between representational art and the reality that it represents. Hyper-realistic two and three-dimensional art may utterly convince someone that they are beholding an appearance that is not representative of anything other than itself. With the experience of such representations, a person is convinced of the objective reality of what they behold, as if it exists outside of their mind and as what it presents itself to be. Other kinds of representational art are less exact with respect to what they represent and give evidence of the distinction between themselves as representations and that which they represent.

Further examples of false appearances abound in our experience, which may include the many different appearances of forms within the dreams of sleep, hallucinations, and sensory illusions. Let us be clear that we understand such appearances to be "false" only through comparison with our standard of what constitutes a "true" appearance. A dream during sleep, for example, may be experienced as a true appearance when it is experienced, though the dream may come to be understood as such, viz., as a dream or false appearance, after the dreamer wakes up and contemplates what happened relative to their reality when awake. That which is considered to be a true appearance is *trusted* to be what it appears to be, giving no evidence of an inconsistent reality beneath or behind itself, so to speak. That which is considered to be a false appearance is *distrusted* as something that is not what it appears to be due to some perceived reality that is concealed, to some degree, by the appearance and that is inconsistent with the essence of the appearance.

It is certainly possible to be fully convinced that a given appearance is as it appears to be, though it may or may not actually be as it appears to be. It is also possible to doubt that a given appearance is as it appears to be, and it is possible to be fully convinced that a given appearance is not as it appears to be, though the appearance may or may not, in fact, be as it presents itself. There is still yet another possibility, known as "transubstantiation", in which the essence of a form, understood as its *substance*, may be established and believed to be united with, although fundamentally different from, that of its appearance through an act of will. On the one hand, this is as ridiculous and empty as willfully deciding, for example, that the appearance of the form of an apple has the substance of a banana, even though the most obvious aspects of the appearance of the apple seem to be unchanged, including its shape, color, taste, and texture. On the other hand, because consciousness must be involved in the essence of every form, a transubstantiated form is, in fact, changed fundamentally, at least with respect to the consciousness that participates in its essence. Among the most extreme cases of this latter sense is the transubstantiation of particular forms in relation to that which is considered to be Divine. If an ordinary form is transubstantiated such that its substance is determined to be absolute Consciousness, for example, the particular consciousness or group consciousness that is involved with the determination is changed along with what is understood to be the ordinary essence of the ordinary form. *This application of transubstantiation may also be considered* in relation to the "incarnation" of the human form, which comingles the particular essence of the human appearance with degrees of divine essence culminating in that which is absolute.

These possibilities highlight the subjectivity of our judgement as it pertains to the reality of appearances, although this pervasive subjectivity cannot logically be absolute, as if there is no standard beyond that of the perceiving individual. The notion of transubstantiation does not seem to correlate with practical experience, yet it does suggest a more fundamental correlation between ordinary forms and the metaphysical reality that undergirds them.

3.2.2. DISAPPEARANCE

There is an experience of explicit *presence* with respect to the appearance of every particular form and its contents. Yet, there is also an experience of implicit *presence of absence*, so to speak, as an aspect of the appearance of every particular form and its contents. The presence of absence begs the question as to what it is that is missing, which must always be relative to something that is not missing. Part of the constitution of every form in relation to consciousness is not only its explicit presence as something in particular with a particular appearance, but also the implicit presence of the absence of that which it is *not*, as well as the implicit presence of absence within itself of the particular contents of which it does *not* consist.

The experience of the presence of absence within the constitution of any form is most acute when the appearance of a form changes in essence through the removal or alteration of its essential contents and the new appearance of the form that is presently experienced is compared to the memory of the appearance of the form as it was before it passed away. The presence of absence may also be more apparent through the removal or alteration of any non-essential contents of a form as the new appearance of the form without its non-essential contents is compared to the memory of its previous appearance.

When the appearance of a form disappears, or when the appearance of the contents of the appearance of a form disappears, the appearance that has disappeared still exists as an appearance that has disappeared, which may become evident to us through our memory. A lack of particular consciousness of the appearance or the appearance of disappearance of something does not disqualify its presence in relation to consciousness, since consciousness is a logical necessity for the existence of any appearance as such. Whether or not a particular being has consciousness of the appearance or the appearance of disappearance of something, it is, of course, absolute Consciousness that is the fundamental Being within which awareness of the appearance and the appearance of disappearance of everything is always present, just as the absolute Appearance of Being is always present and eternally enduring, if only unto itself.

Through our everyday perspective, particular forms seem to come into existence for a time and then go out of existence either suddenly or gradually through the dissolution of their essential and non-essential contents. However, when you consider that a form which passes out of existence has a kind of existence, then the experiential perspective is negated, as this new perspective seems to imply that everything always exists, viz., either in an explicit state of existence or in an implicit state of non-existence. Therefore, an aspect of the constitution of every particular form is not only that it must exist, or that it cannot not exist, but also that it *can* exist in either a state of existence or non-existence; there is an ontological status that is bound to the constitution of every form such that it always has an appearance of existence, which can be that of the disappearance of nonexistence.

3.3. POTENTIAL

In order to have an in depth understanding of the *potential* of any particular form, which is always an essential constituent of the appearance of any particular form, we must understand, firstly, *that* it is, and secondly, the nature of *what* it is in relation to the other essential aspects of its appearance, namely, consciousness, constitution, source, and function. Otherwise, there are some general observations that we can make about the potential of every form. One of these observations is the balanced dichotomy between change and changelessness that exists within and between particular forms. Another general observation is that every form must be in a kind of stable state of reality in relation to consciousness. Both of these observations are essential to the existence of the potential of any form in addition to the other essential aspects of the form's appearance.

3.3.1. EQUILIBRIUM

It is evident through our experience that there is an aspect of the appearance of many forms that changes over time, while the forms exist as particular things, at a rate and degree that is specific to each form and their circumstance. We might refer to forms with appearances that change in any way over time as "dynamic" forms. All extrinsic forms are dynamic and can be observed by means of our senses, although some intrinsic forms can be dynamic as well.

It is also evident through our experience, however, that there is an aspect of the appearance of *every* form that does not change over the course of time, while each form exists as something in particular. The aspect of the appearance of any particular form that exists which does not change over time, while it exists as what it is, we may recognize as the form's essence, the alteration of which would destroy the form as what it is. Thus, within dynamic forms there is always a degree of stasis as a result of its essence which does not change while the form exists. The aspect of the appearance of any dynamic form that changes over time without altering the essence of the particular form while it exists may be considered as unnecessary, additive, and incidental in relation to the essence of the form.

There are many dynamic forms that change in appearance over time and yet retain a consistent essence throughout the duration of their existence. If we consider the appearance of a *tree*, for example, we might notice that the tree changes in appearance through the seasons as it ages, though it is still recognizable as a tree until, by whatever natural or unnatural means, it dies, or otherwise it is recognizable as a tree after it dies if the expected appearance of the tree hasn't been surpassed through its decay or destruction. The tree is understood to be as such by means of the appearance of its characteristics, which are found to be unique in comparison to other objects that do not exhibit those characteristics, and which are found in common with other objects that do exhibit those characteristics of *tree-ness*, so to speak, enough to warrant its categorization as a tree. When the features involved with the appearance of the form of a tree have been established, they may be memorized and used to serve as the standard of comparison regarding anything that could be, or is considered to be, a tree.

Another example of an appearance of a form that changes over time, and yet, maintains its essence over time, is that of a living human being. It is obvious that a person is never quite the same, both mentally and physically, from one moment to the next, for as long as they live. This is especially evident when a person who is near the end of their life expectancy is compared to the memory of their youth. However, despite the many changes that occur within the timeline of every human life, there is at least a constant and perpetual *humanness* to every person as they live.

In contrast to the countless examples of dynamic forms, however, there are some forms with appearances that cannot change over time due to logical necessity. These forms, which we might call "static" forms, consist only of what is essential to their existence as something in particular. Static forms are always intrinsic, as extrinsic forms are always found to change in some way and to some degree over time. The core of a static form is its definition, or what it is in an essential way. In this sense, we could consider static forms to be the archetypes of other corresponding dynamic forms as their less than perfect expressions. The "tree-ness" of a tree and the "humanness" of a human, as mentioned above, are examples of static forms which have a basic definition which serves as the standard for any of their various dynamic expressions.

Another example of a static form with an appearance that does not change over time is that of a *triangle*. Although there are several kinds of triangles and various ways in which a triangle may manifest, the basic nature of a triangle as a shape with three sides is the same at all times; regardless of how any triangle may be presented, or represented, the *triangle-ness*, so to speak, of any triangle is constant. As pointed out in earlier examples involving the triangle, if we were to take away, or remove a portion of, even one side of the triangular shape, we would violate the essence of the triangle and thus obliterate it as such.

Still yet another example of a static form is the subjective human memory of a past experience. While it is certainly possible for multiple people to recall the same thing in different ways or to fail to recall the same thing in the same way, within the confines of a particular person's perspective it is not possible for the person's recollection of anything to be different from what they actually experienced or understood without inaccuracies or a change in their present perspective of the memory. If a person remembers something that at least one other person remembers in the same way, it is likely that the shared memory will be trusted between those who share it as something which is accurate and consistent with respect to its source. However, if two or more people remember the same thing differently, at least one person's memory is either inaccurate or it is accurate only with regard to their perspective of the source of the memory which happened to be different to some degree than that of any other person. Furthermore, if a person remembers something differently than they had once remembered it, that is, if their memory of their memory of something has changed, the person is either remembering in error, or they are remembering from a different perspective which adds focus upon, or subtracts elements from, aspects that were present in the original memory which accurately corresponded to its source. In each of these cases, it is given that a person's claims of recollection are in earnest and that there is at least one other person receiving or witnessing the claims of recollection.

Of course, there are forms with appearances that seem to demonstrate themselves to be relatively constant or permanent as time progresses during their existence. Although these kinds of forms seem at first to be unchanging, it becomes clear after a certain period of time that their appearance has indeed changed in comparison to the memory of what it once was. In this case, the rate of change is much slower than that of other forms to the extent that it is not detectable, or otherwise easily unnoticed, from one moment to the next as the change occurs. There is a sense in which we could call these "static" forms, though they are more properly identified as "dynamic" forms. Note that the repeated experience of such forms in a seemingly unchanged state tends to give rise to the expectation and trust through inference that they will continue to appear as they do. The expectation that a form will continue to appear as it appears, and as it has appeared, is usually doubted when a reason for the form to appear otherwise at a future time becomes apparent.

3.3.2. STATUS

When the appearance of a particular form changes such that its essence is altered and the form is no longer what it was, we might say that the appearance of the form has changed states from something that was *actual* to something that is not actual with the *potential* to be. Conversely, when a particular form appears, either for the first time or after having appeared and disappeared at some point in the past, we might say that the appearance of that form has changed states from something that had the potential to be to something that actually exists.

Forms that actually exist are considered to be real, while forms in a state of non-existence, which do not actually exist, are considered to be unreal. Non-existent forms, however, are indeed real *as* unreal and they do exist actually as potential realities. The nature of something with actuality as a potential reality is ultimately that of an intrinsic form which consists of an *idea*. Thus, an idea is real *as* an idea, but an idea is not typically considered to exist independently of a mind that has it in the way that physical objects as extrinsic forms are considered to do. Since human beings tend to prioritize physical reality over that of non-physical ideas, the reality of ideas is typically treated as unreal, or, at least, as *less* real, than their physical counterparts. The potential of any particular form is an idea that consists of what it *can* actually be.

If we were to consider a physical object, such as the tree in our previous example, when the tree decays or is destroyed beyond recognition as a tree, that tree passes entirely from an actual state of being to a potential state of being. In other words, the tree, which was once alive and real, has become a memory, viz., an *idea* of the mind that is not alive and that is unreal by comparison. The tree that has ceased to exist as a physical object, now exists in a potential state as an idea, which has the possibility, however likely or unlikely, to become actual again.

This passage from an actual state of existence to a potential state of existence is not only applicable to the ultimate dissolution of the essential appearance of a particular form, but it is also applicable to the incidental changes that occur within the process of changes that may lead to the undoing of the essential appearance of the form. When a change in the appearance of a form is incidental and not immediately necessary to the structural integrity of the essence of the form, at least for the time being, the form remains the same in essence as it was before the change, though it is also a new reality with actuality that has come to be from a state of potentiality. By contrast, the form that once was the actual reality, has passed into a state of potentiality.

If the appearance of a form passes from a state of potentiality, or from the state of being an idea, to a state of actuality, which is not the same as the state of being an idea, the appearance of the actualized form must have existed as something potential in a mind prior to its actualization. An artist understands the potential of intrinsic forms through the practice of their art which actualizes the intrinsic forms by representing them as extrinsic forms. A sculptor, for example, may have a clear image in his or her mind of some particular person or object that they would like to represent concretely as something external to their minds, and so they choose to externalize their image by recreating it through the exercise of their art with a particular medium, such as clay or marble. In this case the intrinsic form, which was actual as a potential reality, became actual through its representation as an extrinsic form.

Another example of the existential status change of a form from potential to actual might be the invention of a mechanical device by an engineer for some practical purpose. In this case, the engineer has something in mind that he or she would like to accomplish by means of some form, that is, they have an idea that exists, or is actual, as a potential physical reality, and that is non-existent, or not actual, as a physical reality. In order to achieve the desired result which satisfies their practical purpose, the engineer applies their knowledge of particular forms, including that of method as well as the constitution and function of the forms, to create an assembly of various kinds of extrinsic forms.

It is important to note that when a potential form becomes an actual form, the actuality of the potential form as such is transformed into something with potentiality; an actual potential form becomes a potential form with potentiality when its potential is actualized. This means that the potential for an actualized form to become unactualized and return to a state of potentiality is carried with its actualized state. In other words, the idea of any given form that is actualized is embedded in, and can be abstracted from, the actualized form. Additionally, we might observe that every actualized form is, in some sense, embedded in its precursor. We might say, for example, that the actualization of a mature oak tree is present not only within the acorn, but also within the very idea of the acorn in connection with the idea of the oak tree. Thus, we may have actualized objects, such as the acorn, which stem from a state of potentiality, carry this state of potentiality within themselves, and carry the potential for further actualization of forms.

How do we know the potential of any form? If we have knowledge of what a particular form can become, that knowledge has been gained directly through repeated experience and/or indirectly through the trusted testimony of others. A new form that has never been encountered, or perhaps one that has been experienced by others but not experienced by us, requires our observation, investigation, and experimentation over time in order to gain directly the knowledge of the form's potential; we cannot know the potential of a new form directly until its boundaries have been demonstrated repeatedly over time.

Yet even when we think we understand the boundaries of the potential of a form, these boundaries may sometimes be changed through our own efforts, or they may change due to other obvious or unknown reasons. Through experience it may be found that a person's assumption of the potential of a form was inferior to that of which it was actually capable of becoming. Conversely, it may be found through experience that a person's assumption of the potential of a particular form was grossly inflated compared to what turned out to be possible. Of course, it is also possible for a person's assumption of the potential of a form to be an accurate reflection of that form's actual potential.

It is worth pointing out that sometimes the limitations of the potential of a form is a result of one's perspective or belief about the limitations of the potential of that form. For example, if a person is engaged in progressive strength training of the muscles in their body, they may have a preconception of how much weight they can lift or of how many repetitions of lifting a specific weight that they can achieve. This preconception is a boundary that limits their potential for growth if it is not believed to be possible to transcend said boundary. However, when the person engaged in progressive strength training willfully attempts to move beyond their preconceived limitations by lifting more weight than they thought they could, or by doing more repetitions than they thought they could, the boundaries of their potential for increased muscular strength and their understanding of their potential for increased muscular strength have the possibility to expand.

Potential appearances of forms of a natural origin, that of which are not ultimately actualized through the consciousness of any living creature, including human beings, must still have their seat within some sort of consciousness, as the existence of the appearance of any form, especially a potential form, implies the existence of a consciousness that beholds it. Obviously, particular living creatures can behold and facilitate the actualization of the potential appearance of certain natural forms based on their previous experience with, and intimate understanding of, those forms. However, we should acknowledge that particular living creatures can only be secondary sources of the potentiality of natural things that are actualized, since they are of a natural origin themselves and have been actualized from a state of potential just like every other particular thing. Thus, the only living reality with consciousness that is capable of serving as the source of the potential appearances of forms outside that of human beings and other particular living creatures can be nothing other than that which exists beyond particularity, namely, absolute Being as Consciousness.

Everything possible, viz., everything which has the potential to be, exists within Being in an actual state of potentiality. Furthermore, every actuality that corresponds to a potential state of existence also exists within Being. Many of these particular actualities are dynamic forms which have the potential to become other kinds of actual things and they have the potential to return to a potential state of being whence they came. Additionally, there are other particular actualities that exist within Being as static forms which do not have the potential to be anything other than what they are, nor are they capable of emerging from, or passing into, a potential state of existence. There isn't any potential state that is possible for the static form of the triangle, nor is there any potential state that is possible for mathematical equations, as the essence of these kinds of forms does not change over time and remains in an actual state of existence within absolute Consciousness, regardless of whether a person is conscious of them or not. Certainly, such things may have potential kinds of expressions and may manifest to our understanding as infra-intrinsic forms, although, ultimately, they seem to be eternally actual as super-intrinsic forms.

It should be recognized that Being itself cannot be a potential reality; Being is an eternal actuality. That which has the potential to be is what we might consider a "non-existent" reality, which must exist within a consciousness as such, and it is subject to become, or change over time into, something that we might consider to be "existent". Being, by definition, is within and beyond all particular things such that it cannot be fully contained within the boundaries of a particular consciousness as a particular idea, nor can it be fully contained within a finite duration of existence as though it emerged at a specific time from a potential state of existence to an actual state of existence with the potential to return to a potential state of existence at a later time. Being is pure actuality which contains and permeates every particular actual and potential form.

3.4. SOURCE

We can understand a lot about the essence of a form by considering its *source*. The source of any particular form may be defined as that from which, or that out of which, the form began to exist in an actual state.

The existence of a source is a necessary constituent of the essence of its product, and the existence of a product is a necessary constituent of the essence of its source; a source participates in the essence of what it produces at least by serving as its requisite source, while what is produced participates in the essence of its source at least by serving as its requisite product. Any source is always the source *of* something, and any something always has a source; there must always be a source and ground for all particulars. Failing to ask, or an unwillingness to consider, the question, "What is the source of this?", as it pertains to any particular form, does not negate the existence of the source in question, but rather it perpetuates one's blindness to the origins and essence of the form. Although the source of a form's existence is often considered in terms of an exclusive and ultimate cause, it is obvious from experience that there are multiple sources which give rise to particular forms.

3.4.1. HIERARCHY

There are two kinds of sources that pertain to intrinsic and extrinsic forms: 1.) *absolute* source, which is ultimate, infinite, timeless, non-contextual, and 2.) *relative* source, which is proximate, finite, temporal, contextual.

Being is the ultimate absolute source of every particular thing, although there may be other absolute sources that are relativized within the context of Being. Note that all actual forms are preceded by their potential forms which serve as their basic relative source. However, every potential form, which is an intrinsic form that is necessarily actual in a state of potentiality, cannot have an ultimate beginning to its existence in a relative source since a potential form is preceded by the form of its potential to be, which, in turn, must be preceded by the form of its potential to be, and so on, ad infinitum; all potential forms, which exist actually in a state of potentiality, are eternally without a terminal relative source.

Moreover, there are two kinds of interdependent relative sources that may apply to particular forms: 1.) *primary* source, which is the practical determination of the original impetus of a given form, and 2.) *secondary* source, which can be considered practically as a supporting offshoot of the primary source. A primary source of a particular form is one that has been determined to be the most dominant in comparison to other contributing sources that were potential primary sources before the primary source was determined. Secondary sources which contribute to the existence of a form stand in relation to the primary source to the extent that their contribution stems from, and is subordinate to, the primary source. When the primary source of a form is determined, it is often not only treated as the sole source, but also as a source without a source, as an uncaused cause, and as if it were absolute Being. The same is true for secondary sources that have been established in relation to a primary source. Yet, the source of any particular primary or secondary source can always be called into question, which implies an answer that identifies a source, which, in turn, can be found in want of a source, and so on, ad infinitum. Nevertheless, an infinite regress of questions and answers regarding the source of anything is not practical. Thus, among relative sources, in order to answer the question regarding their particular source, we select the most relevant and reasonable primary and secondary sources among available options.

One example of a primary source is a commercial business or *company* that manufactures products which may be bought and sold in a marketplace. Such a company may indicate its status as a primary source of its products through the display of the form of their company logo, or something otherwise, which may be embedded in each of their products. This intentional symbolic association between a product and its source is a marketing strategy that depends upon a customer's understanding that the source of any form, when perceived as such, participates in the form's essence as the essence of the form participates, reciprocally, in the essence of its source. Of course, the manufacturer of any product is not the sole entity that produces the product, though it may be considered as the *primary* source of production.

There are always a host of secondary sources which support any primary source. As it pertains to our previous example, secondary sources could be various other companies which manufacture particular parts of the products in question under the umbrella of the parent company, each of which may have particular equipment, machines, and methods of production that are unique for each part. Let us notice in our example above, however, that we may question the source of the primary and secondary sources, which will easily be found to have primary and secondary sources of their own. We need not proceed to determine the source of any established primary source or its subordinate secondary sources unless it becomes practical to do so.

Alternatively, if someone were to give one of the products of our example above to another person after having purchased it, the person who gives the product might be perceived by its recipient or by an outside observer as the primary source of the product. After all, the recipient didn't get the product from the company directly, but they got it directly from the person who gave it to them. In this case, the secondary sources involved might be perceived as the money that was used to purchase the product, or the means by which the giver delivered the product, or the environment which served to enable the gift giving, etc. It is only when we inquire about the source of what we have established as the primary and secondary sources that we begin to unravel the primary and secondary sources as such to reveal their position within a hierarchy of a larger scale.

When we search for the primary and secondary sources of a given form through a continual overturning and replacement of the primary and secondary sources as such, viz., when we continually identify the primary and secondary sources of identified primary and secondary sources of a form, we may discover an *evolution* of form throughout an immediate or time-based chain of causation. The "immediate" chain of causation is an endless sequence of causes that have causes which have causes, etc., in which every cause produces its effect simultaneously. The "time-based" chain of causation, by contrast, is a temporal sequence of causes as particular events that occur one after the other prior to affecting a change in the form under consideration. Through the search for the primary and secondary sources of forms we may discover that combinations of forms produce further combinations of forms according to the following pattern: form X combines with what is not form X to produce a new form X, which combines with what is not the new form X to produce a new form X, and so on, ad infinitum.

3.4.2. TYPES

There are two over-arching categories of forms in relation to their sources that can be observed in human experience, namely, forms that are born of nature, which we might call "natural forms", and forms that are not born of nature, which we might call "unnatural forms" or "contrived forms". How do we discern the difference between these two categories? Natural forms ultimately arise independently of human or other creature consciousness, while unnatural forms can only arise as a result of human or other creature consciousness. Note that unnatural forms can be generated by other unnatural forms, and some of these unnatural forms may have a pseudo-consciousness. Nevertheless, the source of all unnatural forms is ultimately traced to some natural form with consciousness, which is to say, something that is alive.

It is consistent with experience and reasonable to consider that what is natural serves as the source of other natural things. It is inconsistent with experience and unreasonable to consider something unnatural, or something that has been contrived, as the source of that which is natural. Everything that is natural has a prior natural source, and everything that is unnatural is ultimately a fabricated product of the natural. Therefore, nature begets nature and what is considered to be unnatural is a lesser kind of natural thing. That which we normally understand as "nature" may be contrasted easily with that which we normally perceive as "unnatural" when these are treated as poles in a non-hierarchical relationship. However, as soon as we understand that the natural is the source of the unnatural, then we must acknowledge that there is nothing that can be conceived as existing outside of the totality of what is natural that is not also some kind of natural thing.

If we fancy that on the outside of the totality of all particular natural things there is at least one thing that is unnatural, then we must trace the source of that unnatural thing to that which contrived it, which must ultimately be something natural. We could certainly imagine the unnatural particular outside of the totality of the natural as having an immediate source in something else that is also unnatural, which, in turn, may have its source in something unnatural, and so on, ad infinitum. Yet, an infinite regress of contrivances does not answer the question of ultimate source as it pertains to the contrivances, nor can an infinite regress of contrivances, or any part of an infinite regress of contrivances, logically exist apart from the totality of all that is natural. We might refer to the totality of all that is natural, which includes all that is contrived and unnatural, as "Nature". This Nature is inclusive of all particular instances of nature as well as all particular instances of what is unnatural, though, as a totality, it may also be considered as *supernatural* in the sense that it is beyond all particular natural things. Nothing is beyond Nature. Thus, Nature may be understood as a mode of the supreme Being that exists within and beyond every particular natural and unnatural form.

Some obvious examples of relative sources of conscious natural forms that are rooted in Nature stem from the fact that conscious natural forms *reproduce* other conscious natural forms which are, or have the potential to be, the same as, or similar to, themselves in essence; conscious natural forms arise from other conscious natural forms through reproduction. A particular adult tree will produce seeds that may disperse and grow into the same kind of tree that will produce seeds for reproduction in the same manner as its parent tree. Male and female mammals will produce offspring of the same species that may grow to be similar to their parents and go on to produce offspring of their own in the same manner as their parents.

Of course, conscious living creatures as well as pseudo-conscious creations of living creatures, can and do participate in natural processes with intentions of their own to bring forth conscious natural forms, but they must always remain the relative sources of these conscious forms, viz., as secondary causes of their existence. For example, a person may plant the seed of a tree and take steps to facilitate the growing of the seed into an adult tree, such as ensuring that the seed has adequate soil, access to sunlight when it sprouts, plenty of water, etc., yet it is obvious that the person is not fully in control of the growing process and, consequently, they do not finally cause the tree to grow. Rather, the person in this example helps to create the conditions for the possibility of tree growth based on their understanding of the way in which tree growth occurs and their ability to implement what they understand.

Similarly, a man and woman may decide to have a child and consciously go about trying to procreate through sexual intercourse. If pregnancy is successful, the couple most certainly participated in causing it to happen through their actions, however, it cannot be that they caused the pregnancy with consciousness at every scale of the process. That is to say, although pregnancy in this example was the result of conscious human actions and intention, the human participants did not consciously control the entire biological process at the microscopic level. As with the example of planting the seed of a tree, the human beings involved in procreation help to bring about the conditions for the possibility of the pregnancy based on their understanding of the way in which pregnancy occurs and their ability to apply their understanding through the sexual act. Therefore, based on such examples of experience, it is reasonable to conclude that although conscious natural forms may serve as secondary sources of other conscious natural forms in a causal sense, conscious natural forms do not fully and ultimately come from the intentions of other conscious natural forms, such as human beings or otherwise.

We might suppose that if conscious natural forms give rise to other conscious natural forms as secondary sources through reproduction, does this process regress infinitely through time and space, or is there an original conscious natural form, or set of forms, as the ultimate source of all subsequent reproduction? We know that life did not always exist on our planet, nor did our planet always exist. Thus, at some point in our planet's history, there must have been at least one conscious natural form that came to be and served as a source of all subsequent conscious natural forms on the planet. Now, we might speculate that the first conscious natural form could have come from somewhere outside of our planet, but even if this where true, what would be the origin of that conscious natural form? If we were to conclude that the life of particular beings with consciousness ultimately comes from the life of particular beings with consciousness, then we must also conclude that life in our universe has always existed and that the past of the universe is infinite.

However, if we grant that conscious natural forms have not always existed on our planet, or anywhere else in the physical universe for that matter, it seems logically impossible that the original conscious natural form, or set of forms, could be the ultimate source of all subsequent reproduction of conscious natural forms for the simple reason that it is something finite in time and space which implicitly has a prior source beyond its temporal and spatial boundaries. Though it would be reasonable for the source of the original conscious natural form to include non-conscious sources of a physical nature, which seem to create the conditions required for the possibility of consciousness to exist in particular natural forms, we are still at a loss as to the origin of consciousness if it did not exist before the original form in some other conscious natural form. Given the assumption that there is no previous particular consciousness or conscious natural form relative to the original conscious natural form, we might conclude that the consciousness in the original natural form has come to be out of nothing within time and space, which is, of course, an answer that is dismissive of the finite boundaries of the original natural form and that which, by implication, exists beyond said boundaries as an ultimate source.

Since the original conscious natural form under consideration is something finite, it cannot logically exist as something that is non-particular, nor can the isolated consciousness of the original natural form exist in such a state. Rather it must, at the very least, stand in relation to that which is infinite, and it may also stand relative to other finite things if they exist. Although we may point to something finite as the ultimate source beyond the temporal and spatial boundaries of the original conscious natural form, or the original consciousness, this source, in turn, may be found to have its source in something else that is finite, which may be found to have its source in something else that is finite, and so on, ad infinitum. The only logical way to answer the question of ultimate source in this case is to transcend the particular source or infinite regress of sources and arrive at something that is non-particular, infinite, unsourced, and incapable of its own transcendence. This ultimate source can be nothing other than Nature, which, again, may be understood as a mode of the supreme Being that exists within and beyond every particular natural and unnatural form.

3.5. FUNCTION

What is *function*? Although the word "function" can have several meanings, we will focus on the use of the term as it indicates the *purpose* of, or *reason* for, the existence of something. Accordingly, the term "function" is dependent with respect to its application in that it must always stand in relation to something else, as we may only think and speak about the function *of* something; function cannot exist in isolation, or in itself.

If "form", as we have been using the term, is *something* with a particular appearance, then "function" is a kind of form that must always be coupled with other forms, as it is indeed *something* in its own right that has its own particular appearance in relation to the form or forms with which it is associated. Every function is associated with at least one form. When function is considered before form, we may say that "form follows function", since form is logically implied by function according to our definition of these terms.

While it is true that every function is a form and that every function must have a form with which it is associated, functions cannot ultimately subordinate forms to themselves, as all forms are necessarily prior, ontologically, to their functions. Since function is logically implied as something that is associated with every form, when form is considered before function, we could say that "function follows form".

Every particular form *is* an actual and potential function, relative to at least one other form, that is an actual and potential function, relative to at least one other form, and so on, ad infinitum. Every particular form serves as an *actual* function of some other form insofar as it is the reason for the being of the form with which it is associated. Therefore, we may ask of any form "Of what is this the purpose?" or "For what is this the reason?" with expectation of an answer to which we may ask the same question, and so on, ad infinitum. For example, we could say that the production of some object, such as a writing utensil, is the reason for the being of that from which it was generated, such as a particular kind of machine or series of machines, which, in turn, could serve as the reason for the being of something else, etc. Every form also serves as a *potential* function of some other form to the extent that it could be the reason for the being of some other form. Thus, we may ask of every form, "Of what *could* this be the purpose?" or "For what *could* this be the reason?". Obviously, the forms with which the actual functions are associated, and the forms with which the potential functions could be associated, are limited in number and kind due to their suitability for their respective functions.

At the same time that every form serves as an actual and potential function relative to some other form, every form also *has* at least one actual and potential function of its own, which, in turn, has at least one actual and potential function of its own, and so on, ad infinitum. Therefore, we may ask of every form regarding its actual function "What is the purpose of this?" or "What is the reason for this?" with the expectation of an answer to which we may ask the same question, and so on, ad infinitum. Using our previous example, we could say that the purpose of the machine or series of machines is to produce writing utensils, and the purpose of the writing utensil is to assist in the activity of writing, which, in turn could have a unique purpose of its own, and so on, ad infinitum. Likewise, we may ask of every form regarding its potential function "What *could be* the purpose of this?" or "What *could be* the reason for this?". Of course, the actual functions that are possessed by every form, and the potential functions that could be possessed by every form, are limited in number and kind due to their suitability for their respective forms.

Often, we may find something that seems to be useless. Perhaps it is something that was useful at one time in its own way, or otherwise something that was a part of the purpose of a larger assembly. However, when something doesn't appear to have an actual or potential function, or when it is thought to be useless, its actual function is at least to *be* in some state relative to other forms, and its potential function is at least that it *could be* in some state relative to other forms. Let us observe that when something exists, it *does* its existing as an activity, even when it exists in a state of potential; the existence of something is its most basic performance. Yet, we find through experience that particular things which exist not only do so fundamentally, but they also exist and could exist in particular ways. Thus, the actual and potential existence of something in particular ranges from simply *being* to various *ways of being*. That something *is* and the way that something *is*, or that something *could be* and the way the something *could be*, always beg the question "Why?" with respect to function as purpose, the honest answer to which indicates the actual or potential function of the thing in question. The actual or potential function of something that is *being* in an actual or potential state as an activity is limited to this ontological activity. However, the actual or potential function of a thing that is *being* in an actual or potential state in other ways, beyond its simple existence, can be multiple and vary widely, though it is not without limitation as previously mentioned.

With these observations in mind, it is important to note the distinction between the appearance of actual and apparent functions of forms. The actual function of a form gives an appearance of itself which is mostly or entirely consistent with what participates in the essence of the form. The apparent function of a form presents itself in a manner that is mostly or entirely inconsistent with that which participates in the essence of the form such that an illusion of real function is put forth. The latter is a case of shapeshifting forms which may occur in nature among various living things, including human beings. For example, if a police officer were to disguise themselves so as to give the impression to others, or broadcast an apparent function, that they were not a police officer, such as in an undercover operation, their actual function would still be that of a police officer. By contrast, if a person disguised themselves as a police officer and acted in a manner that was similar to that of a police officer, although they may fool other people, and even themselves, into thinking that they are the kind of person that they present themselves as being, their actual function would not be that of a police officer. Rather, such imposters, along with their actions, regardless of the degree to which they resemble that of real police officers, would ultimately be disconnected from the network of individuals who are formally vested with, and committed to, that responsibility. Thus, in order to understand the true essence of a form, in whichever way that it presents itself, it is important to be able to discern between actual and apparent functions.

3.5.1. PROPRIETY

When a form is in accordance with its essential function, we say that it is functioning "properly". The essential function of any form is *inherent* to the essence of the form, which includes the properties that participate in the essence of the form, and the essential function is the most optimal function for which the form is suited. For example, the essential function of a *shovel*, as intended originally with its creation, is to enable human beings to more easily dig, lift, and otherwise manipulate elements of the earth through its use as a lever. In this case, the digging, lifting, and manipulating of earthen materials serve collectively as the essential and proper function of the shovel, which is enabled by, and stands in essential relation to, the properties of the form.

By contrast, when a form is in discordance with its essential function, we say that it is "malfunctioning" or that it is functioning "improperly". This happens when a non-essential function is applied to a form either intentionally or unintentionally. Non-essential functions are always inferior to the overall essential functions of the forms with which they are associated. Non-essential functions may be assigned intentionally to forms which have the capacity to receive them, in which case, non-essential functions are enabled to exist as such by means of particular aspects of the form that participate in the overall essential function of the form. If we were to deliberately assign an alternate non-essential function to the shovel of our previous example above, the shovel could receive the application of this function due to the properties of its form as they relate to other forms, although its use in this manner would not be proper and in keeping with its overall essential function. Alternatively, if the shovel of our example were to be lost by accident, or if the shaft of the shovel were to snap, or if the blade were to corrode, or otherwise something occurred to render the shovel incapable or less effective in fulfilling its proper function, in such instances we might say that non-essential functions have been applied unintentionally to the shovel through its lack of essential functionality.

Note that it is possible for non-essential functions which are *foreign* to essence of a given form to be applied to said form intentionally or unintentionally such that the form is incapable of taking on these non-essential functions. For example, we might determine that the function of the shovel in our previous examples is to serve as a means of our transportation from one place to another. The shovel, in this case, is obviously not capable of receiving the assignment of such a non-essential and improper function without significant modifications to its form. Similarly, to illustrate this point with another example, if a person were to believe that their eyes could and should taste food, and if they were to attempt to taste something with their eyes under this belief, they would not only fail to taste with their eyes, but they might also damage the essential function of their eyes in the process. As with our example of the shovel, something cannot have a function that it is not capable having without modification of its essence. A person's expectation that a form will function in a certain manner, or a person's desire for a form to function in a certain way, does not necessarily correspond to the essential function, or the alternate functional capacity, of the form. Thus, it is important to not only use common sense and reason in order to discern the essential function of every form, including its capacity for the application of non-essential functions, but it is also important to humbly submit oneself, regardless of one's desires or feelings, to the actual, proper, and possible functions of every form.

We are not free to change the components which participate in the essential function of a given form that has little to no alternate functional capacity without fundamentally changing the essence of the form; if a form is not operating within the boundaries of its essential function or alternate functional capacity, the essence of that form is fundamentally changed. For example, as a particular form, every sport has rules of conduct that, if disrespected, constitute a violation of the functional essence of the game; if we do not abide by the rules of a given sport, we are effectively playing a game of a different sort.

Of course, any form that is functioning properly or improperly may be categorized as something that is either natural and rooted in Nature, or as something that is contrived by at least one living creature which is natural and rooted in Nature. Every form within these categories has a function that is essential to its existence. Many of these forms have alternate functional capacities which allow for the application of non-essential functions that are different than, but related to, the overall essential function. The application of non-essential functions that have no relationship with the essential function of a natural or contrived form is seemingly endless.

3.5.1.1. NATURE

As mentioned earlier, Nature serves as the ultimate source, or ground, of everything that *is*, and, as such, we may consider it ontologically in terms of a supreme Being, which serves as the ultimate source, or ground, for every particular being that *is*; Nature as Being, is both immanent and transcendent with respect to every natural or contrived form, as well as every proper and improper function that is associated with every such form. Thus, Nature is in a state of constant outpouring of itself into particular hierarchical expressions of itself, which we might say is its most basic and proper function.

Nature, when understood as a supreme Being that is inclusive of all other particular beings, cannot logically be something in particular, since it transcends all particular beings; although human beings, as particular natural creatures, may relate to Nature as if it were something in particular and treat it as such, Nature cannot logically *be* as such. Since Nature is not something in particular, it does not function in a particular way as particular things do. Rather, Nature *is* its function, which, in terms of Being, means that Nature is what it does, namely, to *be* for the sake of itself and that of which it consists.

Nature, as Being, performs its function to *be* both in time and space with particular beings while also performing its function to *be* outside of time and space. Nature is not limited to manifesting its proper function outside of time and space, nor is it limited to manifesting its proper function within time and space, since each of these situations would render it as a finite particular and negate its boundless essence beyond particular things. Nature is not capable of functioning improperly inside or outside of time and space. If Nature were to function improperly, this would mean that it was lacking in some way, essentially. However, Nature is inclusive of all things and cannot be lacking in anything, which makes any deficiency of its function a logical impossibility.

Any natural form, we might say, is "intended" by Nature as Being. Although it may appear experientially that natural forms with their functions dumbly pass in and out of existence by chance, lacking any ultimate design or intention, we can conclude, through our faculties of reason, that they come from an ultimate Source and that they are willed into being by their ultimate Source. This is not to suggest that Being has some kind and degree of consciousness and willpower similar to human beings through which it intends and manifests the various natural forms with their functions. Rather, the supreme Being *is* Consciousness and Willpower, which is inclusive of every particular consciousness and power to will that exists or could exist. If that which we consider as Being is lacking in anything, then it is not truly Being in its fullness and it is nothing more than something in particular that stands relative to other particular things. Surely, any finite living creature with consciousness and willpower, such as a human being, cannot be the ultimate source of its own consciousness and willpower, or the ultimate source of any pseudo-consciousness and pseudo-willpower that may be contrived by extension of their inherent consciousness and willpower. Being must embody and serve as the source of all particular instances of consciousness and willpower as absolute Consciousness and absolute Willpower, which renders Being as the ultimate Source of all forms with their functions through its infinite intention.

3.5.1.2. NATURAL

In general, the proper function of a particular thing in what we normally perceive as "nature" is to reflect the proper function of its essential roots in Nature, which is to *be* for the sake of both itself and something *other* than itself; particular manifestations of what we normally consider to be "natural", as rooted in the supernatural and all-encompassing Nature, must share in the proper function of Nature to the extent that they are able to share their essence with particular expressions of themselves, which may manifest as natural offshoots of themselves, or otherwise as contrived forms. In the case of Nature, particular manifestations of itself could be considered as *other* than itself, since these do not wholly consist of Nature and simply partake in its essence to a limited extent. Likewise, Nature as well as any of its particular natural manifestations may be considered as *other* relative to each of Nature's particular natural manifestations, such as human beings, since Nature and its particular natural manifestations exist beyond the ontological limits of any one of the particular manifestations of Nature. Note that any particular natural manifestation that is functioning properly with respect to its source in Nature may be perceived with a decreased sense of otherness, viz., with a greater sense of attachment and connection, relative to its source in Nature. Whereas any particular natural manifestation that is not functioning properly with respect to its source in Nature may be perceived with an increased sense of otherness, viz., with a greater sense of detachment and separation, relative to its source in Nature.

That which is born of Nature, as what we would normally consider to be "natural", always has at least one corresponding essential function, or natural function, with a range of alternate non-essential functions, or unnatural functions, each of which are possible and may be discovered rather than assigned. If a natural form is assigned a non-essential function which is outside of the form's alternate functional capability, and if this non-essential function is treated as if it were otherwise, the true essential function of the natural form, though it remains with the natural form, is either unknown or disregarded by the person or group of people with intentions for its unnatural application. This foolishness inhibits the fruition of the essential function of the object of nature which will likely *not* achieve the unnatural purpose that it was assigned.

Certainly, it is possible for a human being or other living creature to assign a non-essential function to a natural form as long as the natural form has the capability to accept said assignment. It is reasonable, for example, for a person to assign dry kindling the purpose of burning, at least in the sense that such wood items are capable of burning. Of course, we may go on to ask, "Why should the wood burn?" or "What is the function of burning the wood for the individual that manifested the burning?". Answers to these questions may vary depending upon the intent of the person that burns the wood, which suggests a motivation to gain or accomplish something as a result of the endeavor. This and other such examples demonstrate that to assign a non-essential function to a natural form that the natural form is capable of fulfilling is to establish a *tool*, which may be part of a contrived assembly and which acts as an extension of consciousness.

It is also possible for a human being or other living creature to assign a non-essential function to a natural form without interrupting or altering its essential function. If a person or other animal uses a tree for shade to stay cool in warm weather, for example, the tree continues to serve its natural purpose within its ecosystem while also serving the contrived purpose of the person or animal. One obvious difference between the person and animal in this instance, however, and in any instance for that matter, is that the animal does not and cannot perceive themselves as assigning a function to the tree; unlike human beings, animals may assign functions to natural forms, though they are unable to self-reflect and see themselves as doing so.

3.5.1.3. CONTRIVANCES

The proper function of something that is contrived by any particular living creature is consistent with, and limited by, the *intent* of the living creature that contrived it as well as the essence of that with which it was contrived. In many cases, a contrived object will be something physical, while, in other cases, a contrived object could be confined to an idea or mental conception. Moreover, that which is generated by any particular natural manifestation of Nature has its proper function in reflecting the proper function of its secondary natural source and, in turn, its ultimate source in Nature. What is generated by any particular natural manifestation of Nature is *other* in relation to its secondary natural source as well as to its ultimate source in Nature, since what is generated is not the same as its sources in their entirety. Nature, as well as any particular natural manifestation of Nature, may also be considered as *other* relative to that which is contrived by any particular natural manifestation of Nature, since these exist beyond the ontological limits of that which is contrived. However, what is generated by particular natural manifestations of Nature may be perceived with a decreased sense of otherness in relation to its secondary and ultimate sources when it is aligned with the proper function of its secondary and ultimate sources. This may be compared to any other such generated form that is not aligned to some degree with the proper function of its secondary and ultimate sources, each of which may be perceived with an increased sense of otherness in relation to its secondary and ultimate sources.

A writing utensil is an example of a physical object that is contrived by human beings, with an intention pertaining to its function, using materials that consist of things born of the natural environment. As a contrivance, the proper function of the writing utensil that is in accordance with human intention is simply to serve as an instrument for writing, which may include its use as an instrument for drawing. Any use of a writing utensil for a purpose other than writing, is not in accordance with the original intent of the instrument and, therefore, not the proper function of the writing utensil. We might say that the writing utensil has malfunctioned in the case where it has been repurposed for a task other than writing, although the malfunction would not be due to any incapacity of the writing utensil to write, but rather the malfunction would be due to its non-essential and improper application. However, if the integrity of the writing utensil were to be compromised somehow such that it was entirely, or to some degree, incapable of fulfilling its intended purpose, then the writing utensil might be said to have malfunctioned due to a change in its form, which could be the result of an improper application of the writing utensil to the degree that its capabilities were surpassed. For example, if the graphite tip of a wooden pencil were to snap off through excessive pressure applied when writing and/or through over-sharpening of the pencil, then the boundaries which contain the ability of the pencil to maintain its form and fulfill its originally intended purpose have been violated. Thus, similar to forms with functions born of the natural environment, there is always a certain range of function that each contrived form has, beyond the limit of which it cannot function as originally intended.

3.5.2. VALUE

All living creatures are attracted to some forms and repulsed by other forms. Among human beings, there appears to be a hierarchical valuation of forms, each of which corresponds to a degree of *utility*. When a form is valued, the form is considered to be useful in some way and to some degree from the perspective of the one who values it. A person values any given form as either a means to some other form, such as money as a means to goods and services, or they value the form itself for its own sake, such as a painting or other work of art.

When inquiry pertaining to the function of anything in terms of its purpose is related to an individual person or group of people, the line of questioning in that case is not infinite, but rather it terminates with the individual that holds the purpose as their own. The end of such purposes within human beings is always aimed at the satisfaction of their desire for personal *happiness*. Whether forms are valued as a means to other forms that are valued for their own sake, or they are simply valued in and of themselves, the ultimate reason that certain forms are desired and valued by a person is because it is believed that the forms will give rise to some kind and degree of personal happiness. If we were to ask someone the question "What is the purpose of this for *you*?", in relation to a particular form that they were engaged with voluntarily, the person would be hard-pressed to avoid the ultimate answer, which is to experience personal happiness. Even if someone were to give an answer that was not explicitly related to their personal happiness, the question "What is the purpose of this for *you*?" could be asked of their answer and any subsequent answer until they either stop participating in the regression of their purposes, or they acknowledge that their ultimate concern and desire is to achieve personal happiness.

When we value anything of which we are aware as *something*, which must always be a form according to our definition of the term "form", we may label the object of our valuation as some degree of "good".

When we have a valuation of a form that is lacking to some degree in relation to what we consider to be correspondingly "good", we may determine that the form is some degree of "bad" relative to its corresponding "good" as a standard of comparison. These terms indicate the utility of a form, or the lack thereof, which implies some level of contribution to the well-being and ultimately to the happiness of the person that encounters them. If we ask of the person who holds a valuation of a particular form, "Why is this good?" or "Why is this bad?" in accordance with their expressed perspective, we may receive answers to which we may ask the same questions, and all subsequent answers will, if not explicitly, at least implicitly, point to the positive or negative effect that the given form is thought to have in relation to the happiness of the person holding the valuation.

Naturally, personal happiness itself could be considered as a form, but this particular form has many degrees and can only be pursued indirectly through the direct pursuit and abandonment of other forms. Therefore, the function of any form that is other than personal happiness, as an object of explicit desire for any given human being, is always rooted in the *implicit* desire for the form of personal happiness. If we ask the question "What is the purpose of this for *you*?" in relation to the function of the form of personal happiness, as if personal happiness were an explicit object of desire, the ultimate answer must be some version of "Happiness makes me happy."

Our desire for happiness is a kind of hunger that consistently returns after it has been satisfied by particular forms. Based upon this observation, we might conclude that particular forms are not capable of serving as means to personal happiness that is enduring, much less everlasting. To compensate for the shortfall of particular forms in this regard, we may end up pursuing at least one form more frequently that provides us with a high degree of satisfaction, even to the point of addiction, holding the belief that increased interaction and increased intensity of interaction with our preferred form will move us toward a more lasting and even infinite personal happiness.

There are many forms which can be pursued for the sake of personal happiness, and each of these forms may afford personal happiness to varying degrees. However, if particular forms are not capable of providing us with ongoing and uninterrupted personal happiness, it seems reasonable to conclude that their ultimate Source, namely, absolute *Being*, which is beyond particularity, is capable of providing personal happiness that lasts. In the final analysis, Being must be the pinnacle of the personal happiness that we seek implicitly through our engagements with particular forms, as it synthesizes and encompasses all forms, including every particular instance of personal happiness.

If we inquire about the function of some form in terms of its purpose that is considered to be primarily or entirely unrelated to ourselves and to other human beings, then the inquiry must be directly related to what we would normally consider to be "nature" and any of its contrivances, which may seem to stand outside of the human concern for personal happiness. If we ask, "What is the purpose of this?" with respect to some object created by human beings, we can easily conclude that the ultimate answer to the question must consist of some kind and degree of personal happiness as the reason for which it was created. However, if we ask, "What is the purpose of this?" with respect to an object or process in nature that is treated as other than ourselves and other human beings, and which could very well include ourselves *as* something other than ourselves, we arrive at quite different answers.

For example, if we ask, "What is the purpose of a bird's nest?", one possible answer is that it serves as a protective environment for birds to reproduce. This doesn't seem to be connected to the personal happiness of human beings, at least not immediately. Moreover, any answer that we might have to the question of purpose pertaining to anything that is considered to be outside of the human purview can also be questioned in the same manner. We can infer that this chain of purposes is infinite after it is repeatedly pursued without producing a final finite result, and we will find that it leads to the cosmological when it is resolved, in the only way that it can be resolved, by transcending to an un-purposed Purpose, which is the ground within which all finite purposes exist.